Edmond P. Nash

A Philosopher's Way

A PHILOSOPHER'S WAY

**Essays and Addresses
of
D. ELTON TRUEBLOOD**

Edited by Elizabeth Newby

BROADMAN PRESS
Nashville, Tennessee

© Copyright 1978 • Broadman Press
All rights reserved.

4269-27
ISBN: 0-8054-6927-3

All Scripture quotations are from the
Revised Standard Version of the Bible,
Copyrighted 1946, 1952, © 1971, 1973.

Dewey Decimal Classification: 814

Library of Congress Catalogue Card Number: 78-57069
Printed in the United States of America

TO

The undiscovered thinkers

who may be encouraged

by this book

to set their feet in paths of understanding

Contents

	Introduction	11
1.	The Discipline of Time	19
2.	The Ministry of Every Christian	27
3.	Memorial to Herbert Hoover	37
4.	The Spiritual Pilgrimage of Abraham Lincoln	45
5.	Dr. Johnson's Prayers	67
6.	The Idea of a College	91
7.	The Redemption of the College	105
8.	Religious Poetry	127
	Benediction	133
	Books by D. Elton Trueblood	135

A Philosopher's Way

Introduction

Elton Trueblood is a man whom God has endued with great spiritual depth. When with him, one can immediately sense that this man walks with God. His presence discourages mediocrity, laxity of thought, and idle conversation. Always he is striving to lift the human vision by introducing examples of greatness. His conviction that the human spirit is capable of more than is often attempted is expressed in his question, familiar to his students, "Why be mediocre when you can be great? Immerse yourself in the writings of the best thinkers our world has produced, and mold your life after the great examples."

Dr. Trueblood is a gifted writer. From a literary point of view, he is certainly one of Christianity's greatest twentieth-century authors, being acclaimed in recent years as "the dean of American religious writing." An impressive list of thirty-one books demonstrates not only a consistent standard of excellence but also a wide variety of topics. In all of Dr. Trueblood's writings the reader can be sure of sound judgment based upon sound knowledge. His writings give evidence of his ability as a profound thinker and a trained logician. But his reputation as a tough thinker does not detract from another aspect of his dynamic personality. What makes this man rare is his ability to combine a tender heart with a tough philosophical mind. In this way he fulfills, better than anyone else I know, the biblical precept to be wise as a serpent while innocent as a dove.

Professor Trueblood freely admits the magnitude of his indebtedness to his own teachers, some of whom were true giants. Outstanding among them were Dean Willard L. Sperry of Harvard, Professor Arthur O. Lovejoy of Johns Hopkins, and Rufus M. Jones of Haverford. He was fortunate in having first-class instruction in both Greek and Latin, which have had a demonstrable influence on his own sense of grammar and clarity of thinking. His major literary models have been Joseph Addison, Samuel Johnson, and Abraham Lincoln. It is not surprising that numerous academic dissertations have been written about Professor Trueblood's style.

Although the book writing career of Elton Trueblood ended with his autobiography, *While It Is Day,* he continues to write through his students. He inspires his students not to squander the precious gift of expression and teaches them how to use the vehicle of the printed word. Three years ago Elton Trueblood encouraged me to write the story of my life as a migrant farmworker; I did. The book, *A Migrant with Hope,* has recently been released by the Broadman Press. Thus, I became one of the many contemporary religious authors whom Dr. Trueblood has encouraged, instructed, and assisted in publication.

INTRODUCTION

I shall never forget the first time I met Elton Trueblood. I had just returned from the hospital in late February of 1972, after giving birth to my daughter Alicia Marie. I was staying at the home of Richard and Doris Newby, my in-laws, in Wichita, Kansas. Dr. Trueblood was a guest for dinner. I had heard my husband talk with great admiration about this visitor, and I had read some of his books. To say the least, I was looking forward to meeting this distinguished friend who was held in high esteem in the Newby household.

Dr. Trueblood arrived for dinner at exactly the time he was expected, thus confirming what I had read about his discipline of time. He entered the living room in the distinguished manner of a learned professor, wearing a dark vested suit and pocket watch. My father-in-law introduced us, and I was immediately fascinated by Dr. Trueblood's sense of humor. I remember thinking at the time, how odd it is for a man with his knowledge to be so lighthearted. I had made the foolish mistake of believing that the more education a person had, the more serious he was supposed to be. This is, of course, false, and Dr. Trueblood helped me to learn the error in my thinking.

The dinner was lovely, and the fellowship was great. Professor Trueblood made me feel at ease, and I was grateful for the relaxed atmosphere which allowed me to ask him questions and seek his guidance on decisions I was facing. The evening came to a delightful end when he consented to sign my one-week-old daughter's baby book. Little did I realize that in two short years events would make it possible for me to become Professor Trueblood's full-time student in creative writing.

My next encounter with him was at a retreat in Shakertown, Kentucky, in August of 1974. It was here that my dream of writing a publishable book began to take form. Following this initial encouragement, I made special trips to the Earlham campus with my husband, James, who was a student at the Earlham School of Religion. While James was in class, I worked with Dr. Trueblood on my manuscript.

As Professor Trueblood's student, I have had the privilege of unlimited use of his study, Teague Library. Located on the northeast corner of the beautiful Earlham campus in Richmond, Indiana, Teague is situated next to Virginia Cottage, Dr. and Mrs. Trueblood's home, and just a few yards from the office of Yokefellows International. It is a beautiful library, overlooking the greenery of Earlham's front lawn with trees, all resembling the English countryside. Earlham, founded by an English Quaker, has remained in landscape and architecture true to its roots.

Around Virginia Cottage and Teague Library, a familiar sight is that of my teacher pulling weeds in his rose garden or inspecting his large squash vines. A stranger might find it hard to believe that he could be a man of letters. Far from remaining aloof from common labor, Dr. Trueblood encourages physical work and sees it as a part of "the balanced life." He is not only a prolific author but he is also an avid gardener. His roses are the most beautiful for miles around!

INTRODUCTION 15

A day of study and writing with my teacher begins with worship at 7:40 A.M. For many years Professor Trueblood has opened his study at the beginning of each day to those Earlham students who want a place to worship. For fifteen minutes our thoughts are centered on God, seeking his guidance in the various tasks facing each of us. This time of worship in the exquisite beauty of Teague sets the tone for the entire day. Near 8:00 A.M. the Earlham students leave for class, and I take my seat at the table provided for students in creative writing. Around me are two-thousand volumes of the best literature. These books are divided systematically into five sections—*Quakerism, Philosophy, Biography, Reference,* and *Devotional.* In a special reserved section Professor Trueblood has all of the collected writings of Samuel Johnson and Abraham Lincoln, two of his heroes whom he discusses in this volume. On the far wall, next to his desk, are all of his own writings in every edition and all of the books written by his students.

As I begin to write, the smell of coffee permeates the air, and the distinct ticking of his Seth Thomas clock, which sits on the mantle above the fireplace, lightly breaks the silence. The setting is conducive to writing, and my mind and hand become disciplined to the task before me.

As I write, Professor Trueblood sits behind his George Washington desk and goes over some of the numerous letters which arrive daily. Though this correspondence takes time, he is careful to answer each piece, always in search of a life that needs lifting or a discouraged person who needs a new hope in a difficult world. He often says, "You never know when something will change a life for the better," and for Elton Trueblood this task is his speciality.

In many ways Professor Trueblood's life is guided by the Scripture verse, "Therefore encourage one another and build one another up" (1 Thess. 5:11). His students never leave his presence without being uplifted and encouraged. This encouragement takes many forms and is grounded in his unshakeable belief in the greatness of human potential. He seeks to nourish the divine seed within every person, regardless of age, sex, race, cultural background, or educational achievement.

Dr. Trueblood has passed through many phases—from peace to war and all of the various unsettled stages between. But for all of his activity in the world, he refuses to become discouraged or to lose his cheerfulness. This does not mean that he is naïve about the quality of our religion or the decline of morality in our civilization, for he is a realist of the first degree. But he never allows his realism to turn into cynicism. Always he is able to balance his tough world view with an idealism and hope that can wear out the hammers of even the most ardent cynics.

In the *Theaetetus,* Plato makes Socrates say: "This sense of wonder is the mark of the philosopher. Philosophy indeed has no other origin" (155d). In the following essays and addresses one can sense Professor Trueblood's own experience of wonder. His vigorous spirit comes to life on each page as the reader is confronted by ideas that capture his imagination and lead him to think new thoughts of his own. Helping persons to think new thoughts is part of the purpose of a true philosopher. With a distinguished doctorate from Johns Hopkins University, under the tutelage of the famous Lovejoy, Dr. Trueblood has given much time to professional philosophy, especially in the production of solid books and the promotion of logical thinking. But he has not limited himself to this field. He knows that a philosopher who deals only with philosophy is not a good philosopher. The sense of wonder, he thinks, ought to illuminate the common life as well as the ivory tower.

This volume is a supplement to the author's autobiography. Like it, *A Philosopher's Way* illustrates the figure of life as a journey. This journey is not a pilgrimage along a steep path on which the pilgrim must fix his eyes. A philosopher's way is one in which the philosopher is attracted by the environs as well as by the road. Throughout his life, Elton Trueblood has done more than travel the road; he has explored the wider stages of life. Along his path he has taken the time to be absorbed by the beauty of nature and to develop a philosophy that believes in the high destiny of humankind.

These essays and addresses which Dr. Trueblood has allowed me to bring together may be seen as milestones of his own particular way. The topics represent his chief interests, both academic and religious, over a period of thirty-five years. Since each human being follows, by necessity, his or her own way, we are not able to help one another very much. But a person provides some assistance if he shares with others the growth of his own mind. This is what Elton Trueblood has tried to do in allowing this book to be released.

On April 16, 1961, Dr. Trueblood wrote his first notes to his book *General Philosophy*. These were written on the *Philosophenweg* above Heidelberg. He closed the preface to this volume with these words: "Philosophy, because it is fundamentally a process, flourishes best on the Philosopher's Way. We did not construct the path, but we can tread it, conscious of the many who have trod it before. In one sense we walk with them, but in another sense each walks alone. If each can put up one or two signs, he thereby pays his toll on the ancient path."

Professor Trueblood has more than paid his toll. These writings do not fully represent all for which he stands, but they do help us to understand the dynamic and practical effectiveness of many of his ideas. It is with great expectancy that I invite you to read the works of this timeless religious thinker.

ELIZABETH NEWBY

Cincinnati, Ohio
Christmas, 1977

The Discipline of Time

It is right that the first of the essays and addresses collected in this volume should be the one devoted to the idea of discipline. Christian discipline is a topic to which Dr. Trueblood has returned again and again. In this essay he shares the importance of discipline in his own life and how this pattern can lead to true Christian liberation. One of the great tragedies of our time is the philosophy of "Do your own thing," and Elton Trueblood challenges this philosophy of empty freedom and helps light the path toward Christian renewal. The following essay, written in 1968, was syndicated by the Evangelical Press Association in August of that year.

1
The Discipline of Time

Absolute freedom is absolute nonsense! Though few heresies of our time have been as damaging as is the heresy of empty freedom, one of the encouraging aspects of contemporary thought is a deeper understanding of how the highest freedom is necessarily connected with discipline. Consequently, what was once ridiculed is now seen by a number of thinkers as the price of excellence, whether in physical or spiritual pursuits.

For example, athletic excellence can only be achieved by voluntary discipline. A man must obey training rules if he is to run a grueling race in the Olympics successfully. He cannot do whatever he happens to like to do. He cannot be free to excel unless he lives by a rigorous rule.

The same is true in music and the arts. The young Japanese musicians are now excelling, partly because they consistently practice longer hours than do their Western counterparts. No person can become a good writer of poetry or prose without the utmost rigor. Those who wait until they feel like it simply do not succeed in writing. The world is full of men and women who wish that they could write books, but most of them never do so because they are not willing to pay the price in personal discipline.

Important as discipline may be in athletic and in cultural pursuits, it is still more important in the life of meditation and prayer. After all, prayer is the most momentous of all human undertakings. Trying to communicate with another finite person is a bold step, but it is nothing compared to the effort to get into communication with the living God. To suppose that such communication is easy is to betray an almost complete lack of thought on the subject. The heart of prayer is listening to God, being sensitive to his message, but sensitivity does not come except to the prepared.

Once it was fashionable to sneer at those who tried to follow Christian discipline, but as far as thoughtful people are concerned, this attitude is obsolete. Indeed, disciplined groups are beginning to appear in a variety of denominations. Although the disciplines which they have voluntarily and joyously adopted differ in some details, the basic similarities are strikingly great. For example, there is widespread recognition of the value of regularity in Bible reading and in the steady use of devotional material. The Bible does not reveal its deepest secrets to those who approach it hit and miss. It is widely recognized that Bible study is best if it comes at the same time every day, follows a definite sequence in a single book, and is limited to a short daily passage of eleven or twelve verses which can be read prayerfully and without hurry.

Following this discipline, many are discovering that

The Discipline of Time

the Bible is made up of books which are intended for consecutive reading rather than random dipping. My own experience is that such consecutive reading is more valuable if I date the passage which I read each day. Later, I can look back and remember the conditions under which the experience occurred. What I underline one year often helps me in a later year when new insights into the same passages are sometimes added.

Perhaps the hardest discipline for modern man to accept is the discipline of time. We like to sit around in endless discussion, even when it is banal and fruitless, and consequently we tend to curtail our sleep so greatly that we are less than our best the next day. Once we looked upon this as merely a matter of personal choice or whim, but there is now reason to see it as a deeply moral matter. After all, it is a sin to be sluggish when we need to be alert. One reason why prayer is virtually impossible for some people upon waking in the morning is that their powers have not been restored by sufficient rest. Far from being trivial, this is a matter of the deepest importance. It is an affront to our Maker to live on the level of mediocrity when we could exhibit excellence. Many people ruin the next day the night before, but they never give a thought to the idea that this may be a serious religious failure. This is partly because they have not comprehended the idea that real religion is meant to cover the whole of life, not merely a segment of it.

In the recent past it was not uncommon to hear Protestants express a sense of superiority over their Roman

Catholic neighbors because the latter were required to share in the celebration of the mass, whereas Protestants, by contrast, were not religiously required to do *anything*. They could loll at home on Sunday morning because they were *free*. But now this mood is beginning to change. Is it really ridiculous for there to be something which we do whether we feel like it or not? It is hard to see why. Absolute regularity in the experience of public worship, far from being a mark of bondage or an evidence of superstitious fear, may actually represent a highly realistic understanding of the human situation. We need regular exposure to worship, not because we are righteous, but because we are naturally self-centered, lazy, and forgetful. The more we recognize the realities of human weakness and finitude, the more we realize our constant need of reminders. The more unworthy we are, the more we need the reminders which come in the Psalms, the words of Christ, and the noblest of the hymns.

The person who understands the recovery of discipline is not guided primarily by his wishes, but by his needs and his responsibilities. If he thinks he does not need the help which comes from seeing the faces of other needy people engaging in worship, he is suffering from what has been rightly called "the Angelic Fallacy." If only we *were* angels, we might not need Christian reminders or the regular discipline of both group and solitary prayer, but the sad truth is that we are *not* angels. We are very far from it. Someday, as Jesus taught, we may be like angels, but we are certainly not in that lofty situation now. Accordingly, the more honest we are, the more

The Discipline of Time

we see the need of the help which discipline can give.

As we think more rigorously on the subject, we begin to see something which our generation sorely needs: a Christian philosophy of freedom. The clearest teaching of Christ on this subject is found in John 8:31–32, where we are taught specifically that real freedom comes at the end of a process rather than at the beginning. Four separate stages of a process are outlined, all leading to freedom as the ultimate product. In short, freedom, as understood by Christ, is not something to be claimed, but something to be earned. The first step is to abide in his word. The consequence of this disciplined effort, the second step, is that we become learners or disciples. The third step is that, as a further consequence, we begin to know the truth, and the fourth and final step is that we are *free*. Freedom at any lower level is impossible. If I would be free, I must first *abide*, then *learn*, then glimpse the *truth*, and finally be *liberated*. The point is that there is no shortcut. There is no trick by which I may be free to play the violin, to write clear prose, or to meet the living God in prayer.

Committed Christians are a minority today in all countries, including the United States. There is no possibility that a minority can survive unless it is tough-minded and able to continue in spite of ridicule. But such tough mindedness cannot be produced except on the basis of disciplined living. Therefore the return to Christian discipline is a tremendous basis of hope. It is not enough, but it provides one of the conditions of renewal.

The Ministry of Every Christian

The idea of the universal Christian ministry captured the mind of Elton Trueblood early in his life, and it has never left. Through the spoken and printed word he has challenged Christians of every denomination to practice their other vocation, the ministry. Certainly the emphasis in the Society of Friends on the ministry of every Christian has helped to influence Dr. Trueblood's enthusiasm for this concern, but he sees this as more than a sectarian interest. He considers it to be at the heart of the revival of basic Christianity. In this essay, through verses of Scripture and out of concern for a renewal of Christian commitment, Dr. Trueblood states that being a Christian also means being a minister.

The essay reprinted here was first solicited by the American Baptist Convention, with numerous reprintings at Valley Forge, Pennsylvania. The original title was, "You Are a Minister."

2
The Ministry of Every Christian

If you are a Christian, you are a minister. This proposition is absolutely basic to any contemporary understanding of the Christian movement. A nonministering Christian is a contradiction in terms. The Christian faith is not made up of spectators listening to professionals, and it is not for individuals who are primarily seeking to save their own souls. It is necessarily made up of persons who are called to serve as representatives of Christ in the world, and to serve means to minister. The ministry is intrinsic to the Christian life. The ministry is not something added or a means to an end; it is central and ineradicable.

The notion that a Christian must minister arose, in the beginning, from the example of Christ, himself. Early Christians realized that they were called to minister because Christ ministered, and they were called to follow him. "For I have given you an example," he said, "that you also should do as I have done to you" (John 13:15). Though this conception of what a Christian is was well understood in the beginning, it was lost, or at least neglected, for many years, and is now being rediscovered in a powerful way. The degree to which the idea of the universal ministry is being rediscovered and seriously intended in our generation is the most hopeful single factor in contemporary Christianity. If it could be really understood and practiced, it would produce a new Reformation.

One of the clear consequences of the proposition that if you are a Christian, you are a minister, is the recognition that our ordinary distinction between ministers and lay Christians is wholly false and misleading. It may have significance for some religions, but it has no relevance to the Christian faith. If we take seriously the idea that all are called to be ministers, the old conception of a layman is as dated and quaint as is the surrey with the fringe on top. If we wish our Christianity to be contemporary, we should cease to talk about laymen at all.

Once it was widely supposed that the pastor of a church had a program to put into effect and that the ordinary members of the congregation performed their function by helping with this program. Thus the pastor might desire to promote an every-member canvass and the members would rally to provide the manpower for the canvass. Or the clergyman might desire to have a choir, and the members with musical talents were supposed to help make the choir a success. Though there are still situations in the church in which patterns of this kind are appropriate, the characteristic pattern needed in our time is utterly different. The new and revolutionary idea is that the ordinary member, because he is a servant of his fellowmen, begins to have a program in the world and the pastor becomes *his* helper in order to increase the value and probable success of the program. No matter how dedicated the ordinary Christian may be, he needs all the help that he can get if he is to avoid pitfalls and be really effective. Who should be more helpful than his pastor? After all, this is where a pastor's major training should be applicable.

Illustrations of such personal ministries are numerous and easy to find. Perhaps the Christian is a high school teacher and a loyal member of the church. He realizes that the school is his natural area of ministry. Here is a mission field if ever one existed. He would like to bring as much as possible of the spirit of Christ to bear on his teaching, on his personal relations among students and teachers, and in the general life in the school. How can he do this? Perhaps he needs the advice of a wise pastor in order to learn how far he can go and not trespass constitutional limits. Should he invite students to his house to form small groups devoted to study, witness, and sharing of personal problems? Should he lend books which have reached him and thus stir up ideas? If so, which books are best as starters?

It is obvious that all of the above questions which would face a high school teacher devoted to the ministry of his daily life are both relevant and hard to answer. It is precisely because there are no easy answers in the back of any manual of the ministry that the dedicated member needs wise instructions. He should be able to get some of this from his pastor and some from his fellow members who have tried to follow the same road of humble service. This is why some of the most effective groupings of Christians in contemporary life are now based on occupations rather than upon geography. A modern church will necessarily be organized along the occupational lines if it means to take the universal ministry seriously.

We understand better the right relation between the ministering *member* and the ministering *pastor* if we think of the military equivalent. There is a strong reason for turning in this direction, as the military metaphors of the New Testament so eloquently indicate. The ordinary Christian soldier, that is, church member, is the one who fights on the front lines. The front lines of the Christian cause today are in factories, schools, legislatures, and homes. It is in these that the struggle is most fierce, because it is in these that the real opposition to the basic Christian witness is encountered. Those who are committed Christians are certainly a minority in any factory or office of any size. The person who undertakes to make a witness needs courage, for he will certainly meet ridicule; he also needs wisdom, for foolish witnessing is energy that is wasted or is ultimately self-defeating.

Since the ordinary Christian soldier is on the front line, he needs times of renewal in order to get ready for his task. His greatest support, intellectually and morally, must come from those operating chiefly in rear areas, who exist in order to strengthen the ones on the front lines. These supporters are the men who, in the New Testament, are called pastors and teachers. They exist for the wholly noble purpose of assisting others in whatever particular ministry these others may be called to perform, either individually or in groups. The good pastor, then, is really an "assistant in the ministry." That this is the meaning of the classic passage on the subject (Eph. 4:12) is shown with great clarity in the translation of the passage provided by the *New English Bible.* No Christian who dares to understand the ministry dares to omit a deep study of this passage.

There is a temptation to suppose that there is conflict between the idea of a trained pastorate, on the one hand, and the idea of the ministry of every member, on the other. Some members tend to be anticlerical, feeling that they are forced to be second-class Christians, while some clergymen resent the general ministry, supposing that their own status is thereby threatened. This potential conflict is not at all necessary, providing we have a deeper understanding of what the Christian movement is. If we have a sacerdotal religion in which some can go into the holy of holies while others cannot, there is inevitable tension; but if the pastor is one of many ministers, with special gifts and consequent responsibilities, the reason for tension is entirely removed. Pastor and member both belong to the total ministry of Christ and do not threaten each other at all. The great ideal of the ministry of every Christian is one which cannot be put into actual effect unless there are skillful equippers who guide, inspire, and teach. What we have called the lay ministry needs the progressional or separated ministry to bring it to fulfillment. The pastor becomes truly successful, not by attracting great audiences or by managing large budgets (though these are not to be despised), but when the members whom he is guiding and teaching become effective witnesses in their daily lives in the world. The best pastor is the man whose students in the ministry, the rank and file of the local church, have the courage and wisdom to be representatives of Christ in common life.

If we take this philosophy of the ministry seriously, it is obvious that the task of adult education is a tremendous one. If the plumbers and school teachers and salesmen are to discover and practice their ministry seven days a week, they need a vast amount of instruction and sound advice. They must know how to answer the honest inquiry of the man whose mother is dying of cancer, and they must be able to instruct the fellow worker who would like to pray but does not know how to begin. They must be so familiar with the Bible that they can give guidance, on the spot, to the man who is baffled by Genesis. They must be clear enough in their own faith that they can both appreciate the problem of the person who doubts the miracles of the New Testament and provide answers in the light of reasonable conviction.

The disgrace now is that the hungry sheep look up and are not fed. They will never be fed until the rank and file of Christians are themselves more thoroughly instructed. The needed instruction will never occur if all that we have is Sunday morning religion. In short, if we take the ministry seriously, we must expand our vision.

It is important for Christians to realize how revolutionary the idea of the ministry is. Christ really turned existing ethical values upside down when he put on the garb of a servant and washed the feet of his followers. He knew that words were not really effective and that, consequently, he needed to engage in an acted parable. He had told his followers earlier that the struggle for prestige and personal eminence was wholly alien to his movement, but apparently they did not understand. It was after much powerful teaching that "an argument arose among them as to which of them was the greatest" (Luke 9:46). His rebuke to them for even raising the question was the blunt statement that "he who is least among you all is the one who is great" (Luke 9:48). Later, when the same discussion arose, Christ was even more explicit, showing the contrast between Christian values and the values accepted by the world: "The kings of the Gentiles exercise lordship over them; and those in authority over them are called benefactors. But not so with you; rather let the greatest among you become as the youngest, and the leader as one who serves" (Luke 22:25-26).

It is doubtful if contemporary Christians have given the attention to these passages which they deserve. Because we tend to forget that *minister* means servant, there is always the temptation to reintroduce into the Christian society the very standards which Christ explicitly rejected. It is almost unbelievably fortunate that we have kept, through nearly two thousand years, the word *ministry*. It is so easy for a religion to become wholly dissociated from its roots and deny what it earlier affirmed. Part of our good fortune is found in the wonderful boon of the continuing existence of the Gospels. We may depart from them, but, because they are available, we are always in a position to return to our beginnings and to find a challenge to our waywardness.

As long as we have the ideal of the ministry, there is real hope for the Christian movement. Whenever we return to this ideal, we have a potent challenge to our practices of selfishness and personal ease or comfort. As long as we know that we are called to be servants, we can realize that our religion is meant to be a stimulus to service rather than a means of self-gratification.

If you know truly that you are a minister, you will still have problems and the tasks are barely begun, but you are at least embarked on the most fruitful road which man knows. You will not be at your destination; but you will be on the way. It is Christ's way!

Memorial to Herbert Hoover

With the memorial to Herbert Hoover, Elton Trueblood begins an aspect of *A Philosopher's Way* that is most important. The next three essays deal specifically with persons who have greatly affected the author's life. This memorial to President Hoover is included here because Dr. Trueblood knew his president as a personal friend and spoke the words which follow at his memorial service, held at West Branch, Iowa, on October 25, 1964. Though these words received wide distribution immediately following the president's death, especially in *Representative American Speeches,* they are not easily available today. Professor Trueblood considers the opportunity to have spoken at President Hoover's grave, with seventy-five thousand persons present, one of the most significant speeches of his own life. Thus, this address is one of the important signs along this philosopher's way.

3
Memorial to Herbert Hoover

We have gathered today to honor one of the great men of the twentieth century. His is the story of what is best in the American heritage. He bears witness to a way of life which we seldom demonstrate, but which is infinitely precious in that it provides a standard by which we may judge our relative failures, as well as our relative successes. Insofar as his is the kind of life we truly prize, the basic orientation of the republic is likely to be sound. Therefore we perform a service when we try to make clear the nature of the heritage which Herbert Clark Hoover, the thirty-first president of the United States of America, has represented with unusual fidelity.

First, there is the beginning which combines reverence, frugality, and toil. Herbert Hoover belongs to the procession of hard-working and God-loving Quaker pioneers who crossed the nation in great steps, establishing strong communities at each point. West Milton, Ohio, and West Branch, Iowa, were important stopping places as the Hoovers moved from the Atlantic to the Pacific. The Quaker cemetery near the west branch of the Miami River and the simple frame birthplace at West Branch,

Iowa, are potent symbols of something precious in American history. They are symbols of men close to the soil and close to Almighty God who made it. It is important to remember that the life of toil and reverence led naturally to the life of learning, so that schools were set up at each stopping place along the way. That Herbert Hoover, as a boy of seventeen, should be attracted to Stanford University in its opening year was, therefore, in no way surprising.

The expectation of hard work carried over into the life of learning in those glorious years when Stanford was new. By amazing good fortune the Quaker boy was guided not only into the study of geology but also into the study of Latin under a man as remarkable as Professor Augustus T. Murray. The result was an unending spiritual influence which reached its climax in the days in the White House.

Herbert Hoover's work as a geologist and mining engineer was brilliantly successful, but the public judgment is right in thinking of this vocational chapter as only a preparation for larger public work. The great days at the end of the First World War and immediately afterward, when Herbert Hoover, in his mission of compassion, was the most influential man in Europe, constituted, not an interlude in Herbert Hoover's career, but a logical fulfillment.

All along, the heritage to which he was being faithful was one in which public service is intrinsic. The consciously nourished ideal required every Christian to find, on his pilgrim-way, the life to which God had called him, whether humble or exalted. It included a conception in which duty could be mentioned without self-consciousness and without apology. It required of each person that he should show diligence in his calling, that he should practice frugality and simplicity, and that he should accept responsibility for some unique contribution to the total community.

The most important thing to say about Herbert Hoover is that he has demonstrated an ethic which is identical with that which made America great. There are some who suppose that we have outgrown it, or that we ought to outgrow it, but a life like that which we honor today is the best refutation of their position.

It is not unreasonable to see Herbert Hoover's life in six major chapters. These six are as follows: 1, boy in Iowa and Oregon; 2, student at Stanford; 3, engineer in various countries; 4, director of relief; 5, statesman; 6, elder.

It might be supposed that the last of these chapters would be an anticlimax, but it has not been so. Instead, his influence has gone on from strength to strength. He became the very idea of the elder statesman, writing much, speaking seldom, counseling untold numbers of men and women, and standing as a symbol of moral strength.

All knew that there was at least one great man in America who stood above the possibility of corruption and self-seeking. All recognized that he was one who had never sought personal gain or even payment for his public service. As the years went on, after the end of the White

House days, through the Great Depression, through the Second World War, and through the years which succeeded that war, there was probably no thoughtful person in the United States who did not come to see the unfairness of the judgment of those who blamed Mr. Hoover for what was in reality a worldwide economic storm. In his magnificent patience Mr. Hoover did not even worry about the outcome. He knew that he had been right; he knew that he had been unjustly blamed; by a wonderful grace, he lived long enough to see the time when what had been a problem was a problem no longer. Indeed, as we see the events of thirty-five years ago in perspective, it is obvious that the critics have been more hurt than the criticized. This is particularly true of those who tried to raise their own public stature by seeking to harm that of Mr. Hoover. These critics now stand out clearly for all to see; the public had made its judgment.

The six chapters are now over, and in one sense the volume is complete, but there is another sense in which it is still going on. Herbert Hoover will be remembered as long as the American dream is cherished because he is, to such a great extent, the last of the famous pioneers. He represents the westward trek; he represents dignified simplicity; he represents to a remarkable degree the unity of a faith which expresses itself in compassionate service to mankind. He has worked hard; he has been very brave; he has endured. How appropriate that what is mortal of him should finally rest, after all his struggles and his victories, in his native soil, midway in the western trek and near the middle of North America. He never wavered from the living faith in Jesus Christ which was indigenous to his heritage and in which he lived and served and died.

The story is a great one and it is a good one. It is essentially a story that is triumphant. Therefore it is reasonable that today our mood should be one of rejoicing. This is not a time for tears. This corruption has put on incorruption; this mortal has put on immortality; death is swallowed up in victory. Thanks be to God, which giveth us the victory through our Lord, Jesus Christ.

The Spiritual Pilgrimage of Abraham Lincoln

The address given at the invitation of the Abraham Lincoln Association, entitled "The Spiritual Pilgrimage of Abraham Lincoln," is part of Elton Trueblood's effort to do justice to an important aspect of the life of another of his heroes. This Springfield address was delivered in February of 1974, after the publication of his book *Abraham Lincoln: Theologian of American Anguish.* The words which follow direct attention to the spiritual dynamism of our greatest American. This often neglected aspect of Abraham Lincoln's life has received considerable attention from the author, who has given a good deal of time to the study of our Civil War president. Dr. Trueblood is attracted to greatness, and Lincoln, like no other personality in the history of our country, has been able to exemplify the best that we know.

4
The Spiritual Pilgrimage of Abraham Lincoln

Many of my friends have asked why it is that I have given so much time in recent years to the study of Abraham Lincoln. My reply is a twofold one. In the first place, I feel the attraction of manifest greatness. It is generally recognized that the man who once lived in this particular city is the greatest person who has emerged on the American scene. Consequently, time that is given to the study of his life and character requires no justification. There is no possibility of maintaining a civilization if we do not concentrate upon the best that we know. We are indebted to Professor Alfred North Whitehead for his memorable sentence, "Moral education is impossible apart from the habitual vision of greatness."

My second avowed reason for continued study of Abraham Lincoln is the recognition of the spiritual foundations of his remarkable career. Since, by profession, I am a philosopher, my attention is inevitably drawn to the ideas which are productive of events. Soon, in my study of our greatest figure, I realized that the most profound of his ideas were religious ones. This is true both in his sense of his own individual vocation and also the vocation of the nation. His strongest objection to slavery was not political, but theological. Though not a theologian by profession, he was one in practice. That this is true has been recognized in our century by several thinkers, of whom the late Willard L. Sperry of Harvard, and the late Reinhold Niebuhr of Union Theological Seminary, are preeminent.

Because the misunderstandings about President Lincoln's faith have been both numerous and damaging, it is important to try to discover the objective truth about it. Fortunately, the materials for this search are now available. We are actually in a better position to understand Lincoln's spiritual pilgrimage than were his contemporaries. Our best evidence comes not from the opinions of others, but from the revelations provided by the man himself. A careful study of his letters, his private notes, and his public utterances provides us with the materials which we need. No individual can possibly read all that has been written about Abraham Lincoln, but anyone can read, in a few years, what he himself wrote. Immersion in this brings to the reader a sense of wonder.

The erroneous judgments about Lincoln's spiritual life appear chiefly in two extreme positions. The most harmful error is that of an agnostic. In believing this rumor it is necessary, of course, to conclude that Lincoln was a person of extreme hypocrisy, because no literate person can be unaware of his many references to Almighty God, to his biblical quotations, and to his practice of prayer. In the period following the murder of President Lincoln, the chief exponent of the view that he was an unbeliever was his law partner, William H. Herndon. Herndon's well-known statement was as follows: "Now let it be written in history and on Mr. Lincoln's tomb: 'He died an unbeliever.'" Statements only slightly less grotesque have been expressed in schools and colleges, both North and South, though no serious contemporary historian accepts the literal truth of what Herndon said. Part of the explanation is that Mr. Lincoln's law partner did not know him in his years of greatest spiritual growth, but there is also a deeper reason for the manifest error. William Herndon did not have the kind of mind to be able to appreciate or even understand a complex theological position such as that to which Lincoln subscribed in his full maturity.

The other extreme, represented by several authors writing a hundred years ago, was to the effect that Lincoln was an orthodox Christian as they understood it. The judgment of Lincoln's Christian admirers was almost as far from the truth as was that of his infidel detractors and could not be maintained except by the neglect of some of the relevant evidence. The fact that he never became a church member was, in itself, a serious difficulty that could not be avoided with intellectual honesty. The relative paucity of his references to Christ was another serious difficulty. Though his faith in God became increasingly evident in his presidential years, he never transcended the serious danger of depression. The faith which he finally achieved was one for which he had always to wage a relentless struggle. Consequently, the words which he purportedly uttered to Mrs. Rankin, never became wholly obsolete. To this affectionate neighbor he said, "Probably it is to be my lot to go on in a twilight, feeling and reasoning my way through life, as questioning, doubting Thomas did. But in my poor maimed, withered way, I bear with me as I go on a seeking spirit of desire for a faith that was with him of olden time, who, in his need, as I in mine, exclaimed: 'Help thou my unbelief.' "

This remarkable statement expresses both the anguish and the humility which are necessary components of a faith guided by the love of truth. It is equidistant from simplistic positions on both sides, but naturally lacks the temporary popularity of either of them. The more we study Lincoln the more we recognize him as the exponent of the middle way. He was keenly aware of how easy it is to fall into gutters on both the right and the left and that the only true alternative to both of them is the narrow road. Those who find it, at any historical moment, are few, but this is where the permanent truth is located.

What both extreme views of Lincoln's religious stance miss is the magnitude of his growth. Though some marks of profundity appeared early, we must in honesty, report that there was a radical difference between the ideas of the young Lincoln at New Salem and the mature Lincoln who endured the agony of the Civil War. In order to vindicate the greatness of his final faith, it is by no means necessary to claim that he always exhibited it. There is no harm in admitting that the young man of New Salem toyed for awhile with the philosophy of determinism, which he called "Necessity." The appeal of such a position to a young thinker who has begun to achieve a scientific mentality is easy to understand. Is it possible, he asked, that all events, including those of the human mind, proceed with the accuracy and predictability revealed in the study of astronomy? The crucial difficulty of this philosophy, appealing as it may be to the beginner, is that it necessarily obscures the radical distinction between persons and things, and provides no basis whatever for responsibility. Both praise and blame would be meaningless in a world in which each part did precisely what it had to do. There would be no freedom of any kind.

All of this Lincoln came to understand in his maturity, and this we know because of his emphasis upon responsibility. This is one of the areas in which the great but unschooled man moved from the simple to the complex. This movement, which was finally demonstrated in politics, was first demonstrated in theology. He could not, for example, settle either for free will or divine guidance because he believed in both because he experienced both, and the paradox became more vivid as his thought matured.

The fact of growth was recognized not only by Lincoln's friends and associates but also by Lincoln himself. An important example of Lincoln's recognition of the change in his own ideas is provided by a handbill which he wrote and distributed in July, 1846, when he was thirty-seven years of age. The crucial passage is as follows:

> It is true that in early life I was inclined to believe in what I understand is called the "Doctrine of Necessity"—that is, that the human mind is impelled to action, or held in rest by some power, over which the mind itself has no control; and I have sometimes (with one, two or three, but never publicly) tried to maintain this opinion in argument. The habit of arguing thus however, I have entirely left off for more than five years.

The reference here to five years takes us back to 1841 when the first of the major changes in Lincoln's way of thinking occurred. This was also the year of his most serious depression and the breaking of his first engagement with Mary Todd. Then, as later, his most striking growth occurred in a period of unusual stress and perplexity. The man grew most in his experiences of extreme anguish.

Those who have sought to claim for Lincoln either conventional orthodoxy or infidelity have been able to do so only by the practice of stressing some isolated point of the long pilgrimage and consequently neglecting much else that is relevant. Our task now is to try to avoid this mistake by seeing the spiritual life of Abraham Lincoln in its totality. We accomplish this purpose best if we envisage his career as essentially a journey. There were many steps on the way, but nearly all of them were steps of intellectual and spiritual advance. It was a long way from the rude cabin near Hodgenville, Kentucky, to the White House where the Second Inaugural was written, but the chief mark of the pilgrimage was growth. This growth continued to the very end and was most evident in the agony of decision prior to the last magnificent utterances. This is why I have called Lincoln the "theologian of American anguish." It is my hope that the effort to understand his pilgrimage may be pertinent to our situation in the current scene when America is again marked by both anguish and division. The best contribution of a really great man is not limited to a particular time and to particular issues.

The importance of religious faith in Lincoln's life and work is shown in many ways, some direct and some indirect. One indirect evidence was the moral strength exhibited in his reaction to vicious criticism. Because of the honor in which he has been held in subsequent years, it is difficult for us now to realize how harsh was the criticism which Lincoln had to face during nearly all of his presidency. The harshest of the criticism came from the pulpit and the press, the standard attack centering upon his alleged incompetence. Thus, the most famous preacher of the period, Henry Ward Beecher, said, "Not a spark of genius has he; not an element of leadership. Not one particle of heroic enthusiasm." Writing editorially, the Baltimore *Sun* was equally extreme in its judgmental stance. "We do not believe," said the *Sun*, "the Presidency can ever be more degraded by any of his successors than it has been by him." If he looked at the newspapers, Lincoln could not avoid seeing himself depicted in cartoons as an awkward buffoon.

Though harsh criticism naturally wounded him, it did not break Lincoln, and the chief reason why it did not break him was that he had abundant spiritual resources. Increasingly he was convinced that he was engaged in something far more important and profound than a popularity contest. What happened to the man Abraham Lincoln seemed to him of minor significance, but the outcome of a struggle to implement God's will for the nation was something of a totally different character. He could bear sarcasm and personal hatred because he felt that he was acting under higher orders. Let people say of Abraham Lincoln what they liked, he concluded, so long as he did everything possible to preserve the Union with its inherent hope of a truly free society. In short, he could bear abuse so long as he believed that he was an instrument of the divine will. In this context, he was able to avoid the personal bitterness which otherwise seemed inevitable. In the middle of the darkest year, he said, "I expect to maintain this contest until successful or until I die, or am conquered, or my term expires, or Congress or the country forsakes me."

The hotter the fire, the more President Lincoln found strength by meditating on the divine will. We owe to his assistant secretary, John Hay, what is really a priceless literary treasure as well as a revelation of what was deepest in Lincoln's spiritual experience. Soon after the second Battle of Bull Run, which had disappointed the president sorely, Hay found and saved the little masterpiece which provides us with the very best evidence of the profundity of his faith. Those who claimed that Lincoln was really an unbeliever could say that his public utterances were made for political effect, but the fragment preserved by Hay was not intended for public consumption at all. The sad man in the White House was not trying to impress anyone else, but was, in Sandburg's words, "musing on the role of Providence in the dust of events."

What is most striking about the meditation is that it shows the degree to which Lincoln avoided the temptation to absolutize the position which he represented. His pilgrimage had advanced so far that he did not identify God's purpose with the purpose of the particular army of which he was commander in chief. "The will of God prevails," he wrote. "In great contests each party claims to act in accordance with the will of God. Both *may* be, and one *must* be wrong. God can not be *for,* and *against* the same thing at the same time. In the present civil war it is quite possible that God's purpose is something different from the purpose of either party." Here is the first clear suggestion of the theme which, thirty months later, made the Second Inaugural not only the greatest state paper of the nineteenth century but also one of the noblest of theological formulations. Lincoln did not claim, either in 1862 or in 1865, to know fully what God's will is, but he was convinced that it exceeded in magnitude the will of his own party or even of his nation.

We know much about Lincoln's faith by the way in which he reacted to personal tragedy as well as national disaster. The death of his son Willy, on February 20, 1862, was a sore trial. The blow came when the public causes of discouragement were mounting and when the beleaguered man needed all of the time and strength he could muster to deal with the disunity of the country. That there was genuine depression in the great man's spirit is not surprising, but what *is* surprising is his rapid spiritual recovery. What helped the president most was the conviction that the beloved child was still alive. There is evidence that Lincoln, in earlier years, had a modicum of faith in the life everlasting, but this faith took on a wholly new character in the critical year, 1862, when public and private tragedies were combined. Earlier, when his own father lay dying, soon after the death of his son Eddie, he asked his step-brother to "tell him to remember to call upon, and confide in, our great, and good, and merciful Maker; who will not turn away from him in any extremity. He notes the fall of a sparrow, and numbers the hairs of our heads; and He will not forget the dying man, who puts his trust in Him."

In both of the family tragedies involving the death of a son, Lincoln demonstrated undoubted spiritual strength, but the second was far more revealing than the first. He came, during the second tragedy, to accept the teaching of Christ to the effect that God's care for those made in his image is not terminated by the death of the bodies in which they temporarily dwell. One outcome of the second family bereavement was new confidence which appeared vividly in the middle of 1862 and which, after that, was never wholly absent from Lincoln's character. The darkest year became also the year of the meditation on the divine will, the writing of the Emancipation Proclamation, and the valuable meeting with Eliza Gurney.

If we are to understand Lincoln's spiritual pilgrimage, we must pay careful attention to the friendship between President Lincoln and the wise Quaker lady who was the widow of Joseph John Gurney. There has been a curious absence of reference to Mrs. Gurney in many of the popular biographies of Lincoln. The valuable friendship began in October, 1862, when Mrs. Gurney felt strongly led to seek an audience with the sorrowing president. Accordingly, she arrived at the White House, accompanied by a few others, on Sunday morning, October 27, in the midst of a driving rain. Lincoln had no way of knowing exactly what his Sunday visitors desired, but he valued the Quaker heritage of the Lincoln family and welcomed them heartily. He soon found that they had come not to seek anything for themselves, but solely with the intention of sharing his burdens and strengthening his spiritual resources. To the president's surprise, the little company settled down into a time of worship, possibly the only example of this during his entire residence in the White House. The worship was marked by vocal prayer, by silent waiting on God, and by a brief message from the lips of Mrs. Gurney.

The most surprising feature of the worship in the White House in October, 1862, was that the president himself gave a short sermon. Since Lincoln had no clear intimation of what would occur, the sermon had to be purely spontaneous. In a real sense he spoke out of the fullness of his heart. The result is one of the finest examples of his mature style, the style which reached its climax in his three magnificent addresses: the Message to Congress (December 1, 1862), the Gettysburg Address (November 19, 1863), and the Second Inaugural (March 4, 1865).

Deep as Lincoln's faith was and as much as it grew, we lack, for the most part, addresses which are specifically religious. We know that he gave, in this city, a well-received lecture on the Bible, speaking in the First Presbyterian Church, but unfortunately, there is no available text. All that we know of that particular message comes to us indirectly. But we are in a different position when we consider Lincoln's little sermon delivered in the quiet Quaker meeting in the White House. It is right to call his words a sermon because they were delivered in a setting of divine worship. It is evident that the president had no notes and no expectation of the preservation of his words, but, fortunately, one of those present took down his words verbatim.

The solemnity of the occasion was exceedingly impressive, especially when the president began to speak. What he expressed was the best statement, up to that time, of the theme dominating his thought, that is, that it is possible to be an "instrument" of the divine will. Here, along with the meditation of a few weeks earlier, is a further development of the noble idea which dominates the Second Inaugural. The opening words of the sermon have about them an unforgettable quality. "We are indeed going through a great trial—a fiery trial. In the very responsible position in which I happen to be placed, being a humble instrument in the hands of our Heavenly Father, as I am, and as we all are, to work out his great purposes, I have desired that all my works and acts may be according to his will, and that it might be so, I have sought his aid."

In these magnificent words we have a real insight into Lincoln's amazing spiritual strength. If we had nothing else, this would be sufficient to substantiate his position as a spiritual giant. For one thing, the words, "I have sought his aid," provide the most succinct statement we have of Lincoln's own claim to be a man of prayer. Fortunately, however, this statement does not stand alone but is supported by a mass of evidence of unimpeachable quality.

One of the most striking aspects of Lincoln's experience of prayer is that, so far as we know, it was never partisan. There is no evidence that he prayed directly for a Union victory, but there is abundant evidence that he prayed for all elements in the struggle to be submissive to God's will and for a real change of heart. Thus, in July, 1863, shortly after the military turning point of the Battle of Gettysburg, he asked his fellow citizens to pray for God "to subdue the anger, which has produced, and so long sustained a needless and cruel rebellion, to change the hearts of the insurgents, to guide the counsels of the Government with wisdom adequate to so great a national emergency, and to visit with tender care and consolation throughout the length and breadth of our land all those who, through the vicissitudes of marches, voyages, battles and sieges, have been brought to suffer in mind, body or estate, and finally to lead the whole nation, through the paths of repentance and submission to the Divine Will, back to the perfect enjoyment of Union and fraternal peace."

In studying a noble call to prayer, such as the one just quoted, it is important to remember that Lincoln was praying for the soldiers of the South precisely as he was praying for those of the North. By "our land" he meant the entire country, and this point he made explicit by his adamant refusal to sign his name to any peace proposal which referred to "two nations." In the practice of prayer, more than in any other aspect of his experience, Lincoln included the entire country. The actual power of government did not, he recognized, extend to all territories, but there was no corresponding limitation in the reverent leader's experience of prayer.

The valuable connection with Eliza Gurney did not end with the experience of worship in the White House. Though the two did not see each other again, their correspondence continued. On August 18, 1863, Mrs. Gurney wrote to Lincoln from her new home at Atlantic City, seeking to encourage him by the written word as she had done earlier by the spoken utterance of her sermon. The president's responding letter, dated September 4, 1864, is one of the most revealing of his letters to anybody. We may note in passing, that the Lincoln-Gurney correspondence was in no sense hurried. It was not necessary, at this level, to respond quickly or in a perfunctory manner for the sake of politeness.

Lincoln's letter addressed to Mrs. Gurney on September 4, 1864, refers to the meeting in the White House and expresses genuine satisfaction in the memory of it. "I have not forgotten—probably never shall forget—" he began, "the very impressive occasion when yourself and friends visited me on a Sabbath forenoon two years ago." The contemporary reader can hardly fail to feel a sense of wonder as he holds in his hand this handwritten letter, which is a prized possession of the Pennsylvania Historical Society, in Philadelphia. Lincoln's handwriting is so legible that the letter is a joy to read. Almost anyone is deeply moved when he comes to the matchless sentence which may be the finest known example of Lincoln's matured style, combined both reverence and beauty of expression. The key sentence reads, "Surely He intends some great good to follow this mighty convulsion, which no mortal could make, and no mortal could stay."

As we study this particular expression, our amazement is almost overwhelming. How is it possible that a person who never profited from a whole year of schooling could attain a style which, in an almost matchless fashion, combines both beauty and simplicity? Part of the explanation, of course, is that the marvelous style of the Authorized Version of the Holy Scriptures had become second nature to the man who first read it as a boy in the forests of southwestern Indiana.

As the forty-nine months in the presidency wore on, the evidences of Lincoln's spiritual maturity were multiplied. Among the most valuable of these evidences are the public calls to prayer and contrition, which are more numerous than are those of any other administration. Just before Lincoln was assassinated he was preparing a tenth such call, which, if it had been completed, might have proved to be the noblest of all. His two calls to the observance of a national Thanksgiving include some of his finest expressions of humble reverence. We are so accustomed to the folklore connecting Thanksgiving with colonial days in the seventeenth century that we tend to forget the fact that Abraham Lincoln was the inaugurator of Thanksgiving as we know it. What is particularly striking is that by the time the first Federal Thanksgiving Proclamation was made, in 1863, Lincoln had outgrown any reticence he had earlier exhibited about a frank reference to Almighty God. By 1863, after all of the agony which he had endured and all the divine guidance which he had experienced, his religious language was both forthright and unapologetic. The way in which boldness was joined with humility illustrated the central paradox of Lincoln's spiritual pilgrimage.

One of the most striking results of Lincoln's spiritual pilgrimage is his continuing effect on the life of the country which he loved so much. The motto "In God We Trust," which was originated in his administration, now adorns the walls of both houses of Congress. The potent phrase "under God," which he used spontaneously at Gettysburg, is now an official part of the salute to the flag and is consequently familiar to millions. Though it was no part of Lincoln's intention, as he prepared the famous address, to use the words "under God," he inserted them under the inspiration of the moment. They represent the most succinct form of the conviction which brought his spiritual search to a climax. While, so far as we know, he had never employed this particular expression earlier, there is reason to believe that the fundamental idea had been part of his consciousness for a long time. The exact phrase appears in the address to King James I, which the biblical translators of 1611 used as a preface to their remarkable production. In the boyhood experience of Abraham Lincoln in Indiana, when only a few books were available to him, he apparently knew the few with a thoroughness which it is hard to exaggerate.

The essential idea which Lincoln bequeathed to succeeding generations of his fellow countrymen was that of *limited sovereignty.* No nation and no government, he believed, is totally sovereign because the will of God is superior to that of any finite individual or group of such. The bold translators of 1611 found a subtle way to remind King James, well known for his belief in the divine right of kings, that even royal acts are necessarily under judgment. Their method was to address the king, not as absolute sovereign, but as the one who, *under God,* was the immediate author of their true happiness. The reasonable conclusion is that the boy in the Indiana forest, who studied the Bible so well that it influenced his subsequent style of speaking and writing, knew the preparatory material as he knew the text itself. Finally, more than forty years later, the deeply imbedded idea came to the surface at a time of the greatest possible importance.

The fortunate employment of the phrase "under God"

is not the only instance of the influence of Lincoln's early reading of a few masterpieces. Another vivid instance is that of his employing expressions in the Second Inaugural which reached him first in his early reading of *Robinson Crusoe*. The probability is that, in preparing his most profound address, Lincoln made no conscious use of the words which Daniel Defoe put in the mouth of his hero, but that the expressions were so integral to Lincoln's mentality that they came into use when they were most appropriate. In any case, the man's memory was prodigious! Nowhere is this more obvious than in his employment of biblical quotations.

Lincoln understood that a great people thrives spiritually in times of crisis, and to this end he sought to provide leadership. This he did primarily by sharing his deep-seated conviction that America had been brought into existence for a purpose and that this purpose transcended all self-interest, being somehow involved with the ultimate welfare of all mankind. He avoided idolatry by recognizing America's actual imperfection, saying, half-humorously, that Americans were the "almost chosen people," but it was the power of the vision which kept him going. He believed that God was seeking to demonstrate, between the shores of the Atlantic and the Pacific, a way of life such as to give maximum dignity to all.

It was this compelling dream that provided Lincoln with his deepest opposition to human slavery. His fundamental objection to slavery was neither economic nor political, but theological. He actually believed that God has made all persons in his image, so that each person, regardless of race, is an object of divine solicitude. He knew that entrenched slavery is difficult to overcome and accordingly that emancipation could not be accomplished unless the Union was preserved. Thus the preservation of the Union was, for many reasons, a matter of religious concern. This is why Lincoln's major decisions were made at a level deeper than those of politics and economics.

Lincoln's contribution to the spiritual life of the nation is still evident in many ways. Visitors to the Lincoln Memorial in Washington recognize that they are entering a temple. Now when they go to the National Cathedral, on Mount Saint Albans, they are able to observe a really unique statue, one which represents the Civil War president upon his knees. For the sensitive person the result is a deepening of both reverence and genuine patriotism. In such ways the noblest element in our common heritage is maintained and nurtured.

The conclusion of Lincoln's spiritual journey was one of profundity. Finally, his trust in Almighty God was so great that it dominated all that he did or even thought. He recognized that, since the will of God is mysterious, it can never be ascertained perfectly. But, though God's purpose cannot be seen accurately in the short run, the revealed pattern becomes increasingly observable if viewed in long perspective. Lincoln valued the Bible precisely because of its assistance to struggling men at this point. The Scriptures, he believed, provide the honest seeker with the greatest known assistance in achieving his primary purpose. In his address to the "Loyal Colored

People of Baltimore," Lincoln said, "All the good the Saviour gave to the world was communicated through this book."

Of all the eloquent sentences uttered by President Lincoln, not one surpasses the conclusion of his brief sermon delivered in the White House in the presence of Mrs. Gurney and her friends. After recognizing humbly that, "though with our limited understandings" we may not be able to comprehend God's purpose for our lives, he concluded by saying, "yet we cannot but believe, that he who made the world still governs it." Is there really any more to be said. Here is the end of the anguished search! Such was the faith in which our greatest American lived and in which he died.

Dr. Johnson's Prayers

The fact that Elton Trueblood's edition of *Dr. Johnson's Prayers,* published in both America and Great Britain fully thirty years ago, is not likely to come back into print, is adequate reason for the reprinting of the introductory essay now. It is no secret that Dr. Samuel Johnson has provided the author with a literary model for many years. As Professor Trueblood's student, I learned on my first day of instruction that I should read as much of Johnson as I could. The mind of Johnson has afforded my teacher a vision of greatness, and at no point is Johnson's greatness more obvious than in his production of genuine classics of devotion.

In this, the longest of the essays in *A Philosopher's Way,* explores the prayer life of Samuel Johnson, a truly committed Christian.

5
Doctor Johnson's Prayers

"Dr. Samuel Johnson's character—religious, moral, political, and literary—nay, his figure and manner, are, I believe, more generally known than those of almost any man," wrote Boswell in the Introduction to his *Journal of a Tour of the Hebrides.* In spite of this, however, Boswell considered it not superfluous to attempt to make a sketch of his famous subject. The attempt is still not superfluous, especially in regard to Dr. Johnson's religious convictions and the background of his religious writings.

Though all readers who know anything about Dr. Johnson know that he was a devout man, there are relatively few who know him as the author of genuine classics of Christian devotion. The average thoughtful reader is aware of Johnson's *Dictionary,* of his essays, especially the *Rambler,* of his studies in Shakespeare, of his poems, and of his *Lives of the Poets,* but there are few, indeed, who are equally acquainted with Johnson's prayers. Many, who know the few prayers used by Boswell in the *Life,* are not conscious even of the existence of almost a hundred more like them.

Dr. Johnson was a deeply religious man and a conscious

upholder of Christian doctrine all his days. He was a steadfast, devout, and affectionate member of the Church of England throughout his long life. Not only did he hold Christian principles with strong personal conviction but also he would not permit them to be flouted or treated lightly in his presence. That this was true is the unanimous testimony of both acquaintances and biographers. Boswell says, concerning Christian principles, that "he would not tamely suffer" them to be questioned and Mrs. Piozzi informs us that he paid no attention to the ordinary inhibitions of politeness when anyone depreciated religion or morality.

Johnson's conscious devotion to serious religious thought and practice began in 1729, at the age of twenty, and continued to his death at the age of seventy-five. Though his whole life was spent in the eighteenth century, and though he is sometimes regarded as the arch representative of eighteenth-century England, there is one important sense in which he was not at all representative of his age. The general mood of his age among intellectuals was one of open scoffing at the Christian faith. When Samuel Johnson was twenty-five years old, Joseph Butler could truly say, in the advertisement to the first edition of his *Analogy*,

> It is come, I know not how, to be taken for granted by many persons, that Christianity is not so much as a subject of inquiry; but that it is, now at length, discovered to be fictitious. And accordingly they treat it, as if, in the present age, this were an agreed point among all people of discernment; and nothing remained, but to set it

up as a principal subject of mirth and ridicule, as it were by way of reprisals, for having so long interrupted the pleasures of the world.

Like his older contemporaries, Butler and Wesley, but in a way which differed from the ways of both of them as their ways differed from one another, Johnson set the whole power of his mind and character against infidelity. He went against the main current all his days, and he never faltered. Having read William Law's *Serious Call* while a student at Oxford, Johnson became convinced that it was possible to be a Christian with the consent of all his faculties. "I expected to find it a dull book (as such books generally are), and perhaps to laugh at it," said Johnson. "But I found Law quite an overmatch for me; and this was the first occasion of my thinking in earnest of religion after I became capable of rational inquiry." Johnson's conviction was strengthened rather than diminished with the passage of years. "From this time forward," says Boswell in a well-known passage, "religion was the predominant object of his thoughts."

Johnson's religious position was formed largely under the influence of men of strong intellect, among whom, in addition to Law, were Taylor, Pascal, and Addison. Boswell tells us of the reading of the elegant prose of Jeremy Taylor. We know Johnson gave Boswell a copy of Pascal's *Pensées* on Good Friday, 1779. The two men took with them, on their journey through northern Scotland and the Hebrides, a contemporary book on prayer by Dr. Samuel Ogden who, according to Johnson, "fought infidels with their own weapons."

Though Johnson read many men on religion, he reserved his greatest praise for his predecessor in the use of the periodical essay, Joseph Addison. We have it on Mrs. Piozzi's authority that Johnson once said, "Give nights and days, Sir, to the study of Addison, if you mean to be either a good writer, or what is more worth, an honest man." It is our author's admiration for Addison which gives us one of the best indications of his personal faith.

> As a teacher of wisdom, he may be confidently followed. His religion has nothing in it enthusiastic or superstitious: he appears neither weakly credulous nor wantonly skeptical; his morality is neither dangerously lax, nor impracticably rigid. All the enchantment of fancy, and all the cogency of argument are employed to recommend to the reader his real interest, the care of pleasing the author of his being.

Like Addison, Johnson deliberately sought to follow the middle way and thus proved himself representative of English mentality in general if not of the eighteenth century in particular. This love of the middle way is perfectly exemplified in one of his letters in which he says, "Let not the contempt of superstition precipitate you into infidelity, or the horror of infidelity ensnare you in superstition."

Johnson was far removed from religious fanaticism. He objected greatly to what he called "feelers," meaning thereby those who relied exclusively on religious emotion, and he objected likewise to any extreme practices. "Whoever loads life with unnecessary scruples, Sir, provokes the attention of others on his conduct, and incurs the censure of singularity without reaping the reward of superior virtue." He opposed the use of a special plain garb, saying, "A man who cannot get to heaven in a green coat will not find his way thither the sooner in a grey one." While Johnson was deeply religious he was not a religionist. "Religionist" he rightly understood as a term of abuse, defining the word in his *Dictionary* as a "bigot to any religious persuasion." This he sought not to be.

Though Johnson was no bigot, his religious conviction was so intense that it found its way into all aspects of his rich life. We find his faith in God expressed in the *Tour of the Hebrides,* in his *Letters,* his various groups of essays, in the memorabilia of his distinguished friends, and in Boswell's *Life,* as well as in his specifically religious production, *Prayers and Meditations.* Though always a layman he wrote several sermons, one of them an undelivered funeral sermon on the occasion of his wife's death. His essays were written with the Christian faith always in mind, though it was often unmentioned. In the last paragraph of the last *Rambler* he said, reflectively, "The essays professedly serious, if I have been able to execute my own intentions, will be found exactly conformable to the precepts of Christianity and without any accommodation to the licentiousness and levity of the present age."

Johnson's religion was such that prayer came easily and naturally to his lips, almost without effort. It was normal to him. Describing his stroke of palsy to Mrs.

Thrale, he wrote, "I was alarmed and prayed God that however he might afflict my body he would spare my understanding." How little his devotional practice represented an escape from the remainder of his life is shown by the fact that the prayer mentioned to Mrs. Thrale was composed in Latin verse, in order that he might try the integrity of his faculties. At another time he tried the integrity of his faculties by learning Dutch and reading *The Imitation of Christ* in that language.

All that Johnson did in connection with religion was done seriously and reverently. He would not permit himself to engage in either prayer or Bible reading in a halfhearted or loose manner. "The coldest and most languid readers of the word," said one of his contemporary biographers, "must have felt themselves animated by his manner of reading the holy scriptures." He was equally unwilling to condone irreverence in others.

Central to Johnson's religion was his fear of death and preoccupation with it. By his own argument this was no psychological oddity but was a wholly reasonable position in view of the human predicament. The argument for the reasonableness of the fear of death was put succinctly in the *Rambler,* 110. "If he who considers himself as suspended over the abyss of eternal perdition only by the thread of life, which must soon part by its own weakness, and which the wing of every minute may divide, can cast his eyes round him without shuddering with horror, or panting with security; what can he judge of himself, but that he is not yet awakened to sufficient conviction?"

The stupid thing, Johnson thought, was to face death with easy optimism or with carelessness. He believed in God, he believed in eternal moral order, he knew human life was finite, and he knew furthermore of his own failures and sins. He wrote to Mrs. Thrale on March 20, 1784, when he was very ill, a letter of moving sincerity and honesty, as follows:

> Write to me no more about dying with a grace; when you feel what I have felt in approaching eternity—in fear of soon hearing the sentence of which there is no revocation, you will know the folly: my wish is that you may know it sooner. The distance between the grave and the remotest point of human longevity is but a very little; and of that little no path is certain. You knew all this, and I thought I knew it too; but I know it now with a new conviction.

In spite of this deep gloom, Johnson went on to say, "I am now cheerful." And his cheer, like his gloom, came from his religious convictions. He was able to be cheerful in spite of a deep belief in divine judgment because he also had a deep belief in the gospel of salvation. But his ultimate faith never came easy. He had too keen a sense of human suffering for faith to have an easy victory in his life. He had a great hope shadowed by a great fear, and the fear was never far in the background.

Some readers of Johnson's prayers, noting his frequent request that he be saved from indolence and sloth, may suppose that this was some kind of affectation. There is abundant evidence that it was not. He did, of course, work hard at times, but, like most men, he had to drive himself to the labor of writing. Always he had a keen sense of the disparity between what he was able to accomplish and what was required. Always death was coming on apace, and time was running out. At the end of the highly moving essay, which is the *Idler* for February 10, 1759, he wrote, "The night cometh when no man can work." The quotation symbolizes the mood of urgency which informs so much of his interesting life.

A great part of Johnson's religious genius was the direct result of his keen sense of human misery. Of all blasphemies he rejected most vigorously the blasphemy of optimism. Thus he was saved from superficiality. He understood the Cross. The sense of human misery came on him especially when he was alone, late at night, and that is when most of his prayers were composed. Accordingly these productions are free from the easy faith which comes too quickly to its goal. His prayers are great, partly because they partake of the nature of tragedy.

Some writers have supposed that Johnson's rationality and Johnson's religious faith occupied two different worlds of thought which did not meet. Those who have not been able to combine satisfactorily their reason and their religion find it hard to believe that Johnson was able to do so. But we have his own testimony and that of his friends that he refused to divide his life into conveniently separated compartments.

That he had a powerful mind we cannot doubt. Moreover his mental power was by no means limited to the criticism and production of literature. An example of his intellectual versatility is shown in his original statement about infinity, a statement which is frequently echoed in advanced mathematical circles today. "Numeration," he said, "is certainly infinite, for eternity might be employed in adding unit to unit, but every number is in itself finite, as the possibility of doubling it easily proves: besides, stop at what point you will, you find yourself as far from infinitude as ever." Here is a common-sense observation consistent with the notion that mathematical infinity is merely a matter of syntax.

The best evidence of the application of Johnson's versatile mind to theology is his long review of *A Free Enquiry into the Nature and Origin of Evil,* by Soame Jenyns. Here are thirty-eight pages of careful reasoning, marked, as we might expect, by a rejection of all the easy answers. Much as Johnson despised the conclusions of Voltaire, he and the French thinker were in complete agreement in rejecting the fashionable philosophical optimism of the day. In short, Johnson used his mind as vigorously in his religion as in anything else he cared about.

It is one of the merits of the recent biography of Johnson by Joseph Wood Krutch that Professor Krutch has stressed the great man's thoroughgoing rationalism. "He was too much of a rationalist not to welcome anything that would help make Christianity seem rational," writes Krutch. "But he was also too honest to accept specious arguments merely because they were on his side."

This last point requires amplification. Conscious as Johnson was of the difficulties in the way of Christian faith, difficulties so great that his faith, though strong, was never supine, he was always seeking extra corroboration. Especially he wanted some extra evidence of survival after death, and he long hoped that this evidence might be forthcoming in ghostly appearances. But the will to believe was not enough. Though Johnson repeatedly investigated claims concerning communications with the souls of the dead, he maintained sadly that the evidence was not convincing. Of second sight he said, "I never could advance my curiosity to conviction, but came away at last only willing to believe." Here is the most striking proof of his intellectual honesty in matters of religion.

How strictly honest Johnson tried to be in his religious exercises is shown by the prayer of April 26, 1752, soon after the death of his wife. Believing strongly in the communion of saints, the scholar thought it wholly possible that the soul of his departed wife might continue to be an influence for good upon him, not merely by means of memory, but by direct contact. The prayer begins, "O Lord, Governour of heaven and earth, in whose hands are embodied and departed Spirits, if thou hast ordained the Souls of the Dead to minister to the Living, and appointed my departed Wife to have care of me, grant that I may enjoy the good effects of her attention and ministration, whether exercised by appearance, impulses, dreams, or in any other manner agreeable to thy Government." The crucial word here is "if." Johnson hoped that his hypothetical proposition might be true, but he was too honest to affirm it without evidence.

So far was Johnson from avoiding any direct contact between his reason and his faith that he seriously considered, as he told Boswell on their tour of the Hebrides,

DR. JOHNSON'S PRAYERS

writing a book in support of Christianity. Evidently he had something in mind similar to the book Pascal hoped to write, but never finished. As in the case of Pascal, however, we know something of what the primary argument in such a book would have been.

Johnson's strongest argument for the objective truth of Christianity was the series of events which the Bible records and which have a convincing quality that mere speculation never has. He was convinced, not by ideas, but by events. In addition he was greatly strengthened, as is reasonable, by the judgment of trustworthy and critical men. Recognizing how difficult it is to know the truth in great matters, he perceived that, in many areas, our chief help comes from the authority of disciplined insight. In historical research we are forced to rely on the testimony of those most qualified to know and least likely to be deluded. There is no other way. Likewise in religion, "testimony has great weight, and casts the balance." Johnson knew, in short, that the human equation, far from being wholly removable, is our ultimate court of appeal. "As to the Christian religion, Sir, besides the strong evidence which we have for it, there is a balance in its favour from the number of great men who have been convinced of its truth, after a serious consideration of the question."

Johnson's argument for immortality was wholly from the nature of justice as applied to the problem of evil. There is good reason to believe that God is and that he is just. But justice is never perfectly done in this life. Therefore, if God is not defeated, there must be another life in which the justice, denied here, is finally achieved. "Since the common events of the present life happen alike to the good and bad, it follows from the justice of the Supreme Being that there must be another state of existence in which a just retribution shall be made and every man shall be happy and miserable according to his works."

It was Johnson's intention to be an orthodox Christian at all points, avoiding all the extremes which lead to heresy and error. He believed in the objective efficacy of prayer; he believed in the Bible as genuine revelation; he believed in the reality of free will. "Sir, we know our will is free, and there's an end on it." In his *Dictionary* "Bible" was defined as follows: "The sacred volume in which are contained the revelations of God." There was, he believed, an objective moral order which we partly know, but which is as truly independent of our wishes as is an historical event or a natural law. In the *Adventurer,* 74, he spoke of "the everlasting and invariable principles of moral and religious truth, from which no change of external circumstances can justify any deviation." It was his purpose as a moralist to try to discover, by careful thought, what some of these principles are.

One result of Johnson's orthodoxy was his emphasis on external and formalized religious practices. His Christian doctrine, as well as his observation of human life, made him keenly aware of the fact that men need external reminders of their duty. Johnson was not caught by the specious reasoning of his day about the noble savage and about the beauty life might have if only the artificial structures of civilization were removed. He saw that life without the contrived supports of civilization is merely ugly and cruel.

In all this Johnson was helped by the Christian doctrine of original sin, which he deeply believed. Since man has a bias toward evil, so that even our most ideally constructed communities are tainted with the struggle for prestige and personal power, it is evident that men need the ministrations of the church. Even the best of men need continual reminders of their duty. They are bad enough with the external help which the church gives; how vile would they be without it! Johnson availed himself of the external aids of private and public worship, not merely for his own sake, but as a good influence on his fellowmen. He made it a rule to attend more carefully when there was public prayer, but not a sermon, "as the people required more an example for the one than the other, it being much easier for them to hear a sermon."

The popular doctrine about the natural goodness of men Johnson saw as sheer romantic nonsense. "Mankind," he wrote, "are universally corrupt, but corrupt in different degrees; as they are universally ignorant, yet with greater or less irradiations of knowledge." So great is human corruption that we have no really good thing in human life unless it is artfully contrived. The way out, therefore, lies not in despising the help which the Bible and church can give, but in using them as incentives.

Man is such a creature that he dare not neglect any individual "incitement to do well." This is because we are men and not angels.

Johnson's concern for the externals of religion is shown in his respect for the day of rest and for his religious employment of various important days of the year which served as reminders. The first of the three things he required of Sir Joshua Reynolds was that Reynolds would promise not to work on Sundays, and the second was that the painter would read a portion of Scripture each Sunday. He deplored the nonobservance of Good Friday. So great was Johnson's indolence that in spite of his theories and his advice he was not wholly regular in such practices himself. Though he was sure that Sunday observance was one of the chief buttresses of civilization, he made it clear that he opposed any tendency to keep the day with rigid severity and gloom. What he valued, as a support for the best in human life, was the rhythm of the week rather than dull monotony, and he prized the sabbath because it provided for mankind this beneficent rhythm. "It should be different from another day," he told Boswell on their famous tour. The Sundays which he passed at home, according to Sir John Hawkins, were "spent in the private exercises of devotion, and sanctified by acts of charity of a singular kind: on that day he accepted of no invitation abroad, but gave a dinner to such of his poor friends as might else have gone without one."

In the last year of his life, Dr. Johnson had a serious conversation with Dr. Adams of Oxford on the subject of the production of a book of prayers. To the request that he compose some family prayers, Johnson replied, "I will not compose prayers for you, Sir, because you can do it for yourself." After this characteristic blast, the great man went on, "But I have thought of getting together all the books of prayers which I could, selecting those which should appear to me the best, pulling out some, inserting others, adding some prayers of my own, and prefixing a discourse on prayer." Not only did Johnson entertain such a plan but also he was actually offered, says Boswell, a large sum for a volume of devotional exercises. It is unfortunate that this, like many of Johnson's other plans, was never executed. But there is some satisfaction that so many of the actual prayers were saved from destruction when most of the intimate papers were destroyed. The collection now printed constitutes the closest approximation we can make to Johnson's intended volume on prayer.

Though the idea of producing a prayer book seems to have come late in Johnson's life, he had been writing devotional literature for many years. This literature consisted partly of prayers and partly of the author's comments on his own spiritual condition or resolutions to do better. He was inspired, more than most men, by recurring anniversaries, such as those of his own birth, his wife's death, the beginning of the year, and Easter. The first prayer he wrote was a birthday prayer in 1738. He was also moved to devotional writing by any new undertaking of a serious character, such as the *Rambler* in 1750 or the study of law in 1765. Just before he died, Johnson put all of this highly personal material together and, because he was too ill to edit it himself, handed the lot to the Reverend George Strahan, with permission to publish. Dr. Strahan undertook the laborious task of getting Johnson's unedited devotional manuscripts ready for publication and finally brought out a faithful reproduction of the material in 1785, under the title *Prayers and Devotions.* Because he feared that the authenticity of the work might be doubted, Dr. Strahan deposited the manuscripts in the library of Pembroke College, Oxford, where they remain. The present editor has had the privilege of using these manuscripts, which are well preserved. They appear on sheets of many shapes and sizes and show only the beginnings of classification.

That Dr. Strahan's decision was a difficult one is clear. Though many of the journal items were almost worthless and many of them highly repetitious, the editor of the posthumous work decided to publish everything and to arrange all, whether prayers or diaries, merely by reference to the time of writing. He was undoubtedly influenced in this course by the fact that, in the Pembroke manuscripts, some of the prayers are already imbedded in other matter. Though one can understand the basis of Dr. Strahan's decision, it remains true that this decision has not proved a wholly fortunate one.

The inclusion of all of the journal items along with the prayers, as is done in the *Collected Works,* and in Volume I of Birkbeck Hill's *Johnsonian Miscellanies,* is not fair to Johnson. Whereas the prayers are highly polished productions, the autobiographical fragments are not. Some of them are so intimate in reference that it is hard to believe Johnson expected them to be published. We must remember that he was an old and ill man when he handed the manuscripts to his friend. When we recall that some of the most unfavorable judgments of Dr. Johnson's character and religion, particularly those relating to his fear of death, have come from this source, it is not surprising that several of his closest friends were resentful that Dr. Strahan had allowed the work to appear. The inclusion of the journal items was more unfortunate still in the fact that it kept the prayers from appearing in their true glory. This is undoubtedly the chief reason why so many well-read people are surprised to learn that Johnson was the author of prayers at all.

The purpose of this volume is to allow the prayers to stand alone, with no encumbrances, so that they may become better known and consequently better loved. I have added captions to facilitate easy reference, but wherever possible, these captions retain and employ Johnson's own phrases, as found in his appended notes.

In order to make the prayers more useful and to keep closer to Johnson's own original purpose, I have classified the prayers according to eight major categories and have added, at the end, the last of all Dr. Johnson's many writings, the prayer which he wrote just before he died, the manuscript of which is in the possession of Professor Chauncey B. Tinker of Yale University. The notation on the manuscripts leads one to believe that, had Johnson lived to edit his own work, he would have classified the prayers according to some such categories of human need as have been employed in the present volume. Within each major classification the chronological order has been preserved, wherever this is known.

Though the purpose of the present book is that of making Johnson's devotional classics available to modern readers, and is therefore not merely antiquarian, it has seemed best, nevertheless, to retain the peculiar punctuation and capitalization of the original manuscripts. These help to bring the reader closer to the eighteenth-century author. The fact that Johnson did not live to give these details the merit of consistency presents no serious problem to the modern reader.

The manuscripts of the prayers provide a remarkable revelation of important features of Dr. Johnson's character. Most of them show signs of much correction, both in thought and in style, the rejected phrases being, in some cases, so heavily blacked out that it is not possible to recover them. On the manuscript of the famour prayer on the *Rambler* the ejaculations "Lord help me" and "So be it" appear underneath the main text, but have been crossed out. Below the birthday prayer for September 18, 1758, Johnson wrote: "This year I hope to learn diligence."

Several of the prayers give the hour as well as the date of composition, most of them indicating hours in the middle of the night. The prayer for January 1, 1749/50 was composed "After three in the morning," while the birthday prayer for 1775, was written during "a sleepless night." Information about Johnson's general religious practices is provided by some of the manuscripts, as when the note appended to the Easter prayer for 1753 says: "This I repeated sometimes at Church."

Several of the prayers were evidently written more than once and sometimes the development of thought and style can be traced. Thus we find, on the back of the manuscript of the prayer for March 24, 1759, the following, which is apparently an earlier form of the prayer listed in the present collection under the caption "Change of Circumstances."

> O Lord, let the change which I am now making in outward things produce in me such a change of manners, as may fit me (for) the great change through which my wife has passed.

It is hard to overestimate the enormous influence on Johnson of the death of his wife in March 1752. This influence appears in many of his literary productions, but most vividly in his devotional writings. Whereas the numbers of the *Rambler* ended with Mrs. Johnson's death, the production of devotional writings was greatly accentuated by this sad occurrence. Of the one hundred previous prayers printed in the present collection, only *five* were written before Mrs. Johnson died. All the Easter prayers were written after her death, the doctor's meticulous care in the celebration of Easter throughout the remaining thirty-two years of his life being occasioned by his conviction that such care was in accordance with his deceased mate's wish.

Any sensitive reader is bound to be deeply moved by the way in which Johnson remembered his wife, turning his personal sorrow into a means of spiritual growth. In doing so he has given a worthy example to all who suffer bereavement and loneliness. The journal entry for Good Friday, March 28, 1777, says, "I remembered that it was my wife's dying day, and begged pardon for all our sins, and commended her: but resolved to mix little of my own sorrows or cares with the great solemnity."

How little the years dimmed his grief is shown by a journal entry five years later. "This is the day on which in 1752 dear Tetty died," he wrote. "We were married almost seventeen years, and have now been parted thirty." In view of the genuineness of his grief and the greatness of the man, there is reason to doubt the fairness of contemporary estimates of Mrs. Johnson which have long made the world think poorly of her. That she was not perfect the doctor recognized. Even in one of the most moving of his prayers, that written four weeks after she died, he prayed not only that he might "imitate whatever was in her life acceptable," but also that he might "avoid all by which she offended." The bereaved man, we conclude, was aware in his wife's character of admirable traits unknown to those who did not love her.

It will generally be agreed that it is in those petitions penned by Johnson soon after his bereavement that he reached the greatest heights. It is hard to think of any prayer in our language which states so perfectly what a devout man may feel in sorrow as that written on May 6, 1752. It appears in this volume under the caption "After Thirty-nine Days." The petition "that neither praise may fill me with pride, nor censure with discontent" represents at its best Johnson's remarkable felicity of phrase.

The prayers as they now appear are *genuine classics of devotion*. This is shown both by their content and by their form. The form, for the most part, is that of the "Collect," the form most demonstrated in the *Book of Common Prayer*. Trained from childhood in the use of this form, Johnson was conscious of standing in a noble tradition and added materially to it. The collect form is a reasonably strict one, proceeding from salutation to ascription, to petition, to reason for petition, to conclusion. The whole is marked by a singular economy of phrase which permits neither padding nor digression. The Johnson prayers which show the most meticulous collect style are the "Introductory Prayer," written March 25, 1756, and the prayer on Volume II of the *Dictionary*, composed April 3, 1753. All the known prayers written by Johnson are included in this edition.

One of the most moving of the prayers in this volume was made at the bedside of his mother's maid, Kitty Chambers, as the serving woman lay dying. The journal entry for Sunday, October 18, 1767, is as follows:

> Yesterday, Oct. 17, at about ten in the morning I took my leave for ever of my dear old friend, Catherine Chambers, who came to live with my mother about 1724, and has been but little parted from us since. She buried my father, my brother, and my mother. She is now fifty-eight years old. I desired all to withdraw, then told her that we were to part forever, that as Christians, we should

> part with prayer; and that I would, if she was willing, say a short prayer beside her. She expressed great desire to hear me; and held up her poor hands, as she lay in bed, with great fervour, while I prayed kneeling by her. . . . I then kissed her. She told me that to part was the greatest pain she had ever felt, and that she hoped we should meet again in a better place. I expressed with swelled eyes, and great emotion of tenderness, the same hopes. We kissed, and parted. I humbly hope to meet again and part no more.

Here is one of the truly noble scenes of our history—the leading man of letters of his nation and century kneeling, in humble faith, by the bedside of his mother's servant. The worship of God broke down all distinctions of rank, no matter how important they might seem on other grounds. Johnson was made humble in the only way a man of his stubborn intellectual pride could be made humble, by an overwhelming sense of the reality of God which made him see his own life in its true light.

In the prayers printed on the pages of this book, the reader may gain some insight into the character of a man who was marked above all by a rugged honesty which made him face repeatedly his own failures. Because such failure is a common human experience, uniting all men, even though they live in different centuries, and because the faith in God which is the ultimate reason for these prayers is independent of changing fashions, these noble words written in one century may speak to the condition of perplexed men and women living in the middle of another.

The Idea of a College

This 1949 address, delivered to the Association of American Colleges, was expanded into a book of the same title, *The Idea of a College,* which is now out of print. The dream of what a Christian college might be has deeply influenced Dr. Trueblood's mind and has led him to spend nearly all of his career on one college campus or another. It is, therefore, highly appropriate that Professor Trueblood and Mrs. Trueblood built their own retirement home on the campus of Earlham, the college he has served longer than any other.

Dr. Trueblood views the college as more than just a place to get a degree so that one can secure a job. For him, the college is nothing less than "a conscious effort to avoid the decay of civilization and to make that civilization worthy of permanence." In this essay, the author tells how we can create, in colleges across the country, "islands of hope in the midst of a century of despair."

6
The Idea of a College

The most sobering thought that comes to the attention of modern students is the thought that civilizations can pass away. It is a shocking thing for a young person to realize that in parts of North Africa and in parts of western Asia there are now only shifting sands where once there were prosperous and educated populations. The really thoughtful student immediately makes the deduction that our own boasted civilization can likewise perish and that it *will* perish unless a great deal of concerned intelligence is devoted to its preservation. Great as our present wealth and security may be, they are not necessarily permanent.

Now a college, whatever else it may be, is a conscious effort to avoid the decay of civilization and to make that civilization worthy of permanence. Knowing that we are in danger, we have contrived means by which the improvement of civilization may be undertaken. The institution of higher education may be compared to a pumping station on a pipeline. In the great lines from Texas to the northern states we cannot rely on gravity, even when the pipes go downhill, for that is too slow. We must have some means of boosting this process. Places of learning are similarly spaced in our culture and devoted to a similar function.

We are tempted, sometimes, to lump all education together and call it good, saying vaguely that education is what we need. Most of us now are more critical than this because we realize that education, like religion, can be both good and bad. Religion is not necessarily good and neither is education if we are to judge by the general effect on human lives. We have to admit that much of our present education, including what is rather hopefully called higher education, is actually shoddy. Not all degrees are equally valuable, whatever the public may think, and not all colleges are equally concerned with the central task before them. That is one reason why meetings like this are valuable; we must help each other continually to know what the main task is and how to perform it effectively.

All will likewise agree that there is frequently a great difference between our theory and our practice. All education sounds wonderful in college catalogs. There is very little wrong with the catalogs; what we require is some factual resemblance to what they say. Last year I visited more than thirty colleges and universities in this nation, and I was frankly dismayed at much that I saw. One result was an address at Denison which, to my surprise, was quoted on the editorial page of *Life.* I was surprised because what I said seemed to me a commonplace among those concerned with the actual practice of academic institutions. What I said was that we are graduating people who can barely read and that thousands of those who *can* read, appear to have no standards of excellence about *what* to read. It was and is my conviction that the majority of those who emerge from American institutions of higher learning today have no real sense of life's meaning, and many of them are not vitally concerned with finding any. The great majority, whatever their technological skills, have no grasp of the Judeo-Christian roots of democracy. Much of the same report was made by Sir Richard Livingstone when he said, "The influence of universities on the world is disappointingly limited."

In the face of such confusion and relative failure it is necessary, from time to time, that we know what and where we are. We must reset out compasses. We must know what we are before we can know our duty. Almost a century ago John Henry Newman wrote the remarkable lecture-essays to which he gave the title, "The Idea of a University." Now, in the middle of this century, we must go on to explore "The Idea of a College." We need this because we are often so vague in our references and almost meaningless in our classifications.

One almost meaningless distinction is between public and private institutions. The usual suggestion here is that the tax-supported institution is public, whereas the others are private. But a little thought should make us realize that public responsibility and public service depend neither on the way funds are raised nor on the way boards are appointed. The institutions which I have served in my teaching career, Guilford, Haverford, Stanford, and Earlham, have never, so far as I know, received directly one cent of tax money, but they are definitely public in the way they perform their functions. There *could* be a private institution run for profit or for the welfare of a specialized group, but this is not the direction in which we have sought to go. If we are to make a distinction, let it be between governmental institutions and independent foundations.

Even greater confusion is shown in our use of the terms *college* and *university*. Often it has been the ambition of colleges to cease to be colleges and become universities. This is on the assumption that a university is bigger and that bigger things are *eo ipso* better. I am afraid that a good many of our citizens think that a university is a *large* or *prosperous* or *ambitious* college. This, of course, we must challenge. It is undoubtedly true that we can, if we choose, emulate Humpty Dumpty in his famous conversation with Alice over the meaning of the word *glory.* "When I use a word," Humpty Dumpty said in rather a scornful tone, "it means just what I choose it to mean— neither more nor less." But in our less arbitrary world of normal experience, it is right to have some decent regard to what words have meant before. Historically, it has been agreed that a university is a place of universal knowledge or a collection of colleges. A college, on the other hand, has no necessity of being a place of universal knowledge, for it is primarily a place of *teaching. A college is a society.* It is made up of learners and teachers living together for the purpose of human growth. The purpose of a college determines its size and a really large college is a contradiction in terms since the community experience which is basic to the idea is then impossible. A college is a contrived means of bringing to bear maximum beneficent influence to produce maximum progress in the individuals concerned. Ideally, the members of a college, both teachers and taught, *work* together, *think* together, *play* together, and *pray* together. We must not let our praying remain separate from our thinking or our playing be wholly dissociated from our working. It is the wholeness of life that we consciously and deliberately seek.

It is essential to the idea of a college that the contacts between members outside the lecture room or laboratory may be the most effective of all instruments of growth and are in no sense peripheral. The late Professor Whitehead, one of the best-educated men of our time, has told us that, while an undergraduate at Cambridge, he never heard lectures on any subject except mathematics. Where then did he get his extraordinary interest in philosophy, in history, and in letters? He got all this, he tells us, by the conversations in the dining hall where he often sat from six to ten, learning rapidly, not only from his equals but also from his elders and betters. When we think of the eat-and-run procedure of so much of our modern dining, we understand one of our chief sources of failure. It is possible that the invention of the college cafeteria has done more to destroy culture than any other device of the adversary. I wish it were part of every instructor's responsibility to dine in the cafeteria at least once a week.

Partly because of unfavorable publicity about crimes in educational institutions and partly by analysis of our total contemporary predicament, we realize that in our colleges we cannot sidestep the question of moral influence. The sad and unpleasant truth is that some students are made *worse* by going to college, and sometimes it seems that *many* are. There are institutions where self-sacrificing parents are being cheated, for they send their young people with high hopes, little knowing that in some instances their children are being thrown into a situation where the pressure in the direction of downright immorality is terrible.

We need to give intelligent thought to the whole question of moral progress and, fortunately, the main lines here are rather clear. We know that growth in decency and integrity come chiefly, not by direct moral teaching, but rather by general atmosphere, by fellowship in creative work and by firsthand acquaintance with great minds, great books, and great art. Perhaps the wisest of all the wisest sayings of Professor Whitehead was this: "Moral progress is impossible apart from the habitual vision of greatness." Here, if anywhere, is a golden text! Our students need to be saved from triviality, but they don't even know what *is* trivial until they have a vision of greatness to make the contrast clear. Think what it means to put before young people a great towering figure like John R. Mott, holder of the Nobel prize for peace or a man like Albert Einstein. If we can provide our students with a steady stream of such experiences, we have done for them the best that we shall ever do. Remember that isolated experience will not ordinarily suffice. Men are lifted when the vision of greatness is *habitual.*

From moral education we move naturally to the place of religion in a college. Of this we may be sure, we must have religion in college, for otherwise we are not concerned with the creation of wholeness. What both students and professors need is the reverence and the commitment to the living God that can give power to their moral aspirations. Ideally the religion should not be a *part* of the college, but rather an atmosphere of reverence which pervades the entire enterprise. As my colleague, William Clark, has so well said, "The Christian College does not *have* a religious program; it *is* a religious program."

If the religious program is to be a healthy one, there must be a continual outflow of energy from the campus. A campus religious organization which exists only for the profit of its own members is already dead, but it may be living if it has an outlet in deputations, in service projects, and in a variety of community contacts.

Historically, the college chapel has been the chief college symbol and the focal point of all meaning. Now, unfortunately, this is often greatly changed and many college presidents admit frankly that they do not know what to do with chapel. In many places we are beating a more or less steady retreat because the life seems to have gone out of what was once noble. I think the way of wisdom here is to take a firm stand, reverse the process of erosion, and make the chapel central again. Otherwise we become fragmented and cease to be organic communities. I think it is wise to make a clearcut distinction between assemblies and college chapels, to make the former frankly secular and to make the latter unapologetically devout. Above all, we must make them *good,* and we must be willing to spend the time, effort, and money to achieve this end. In my own college we probably put more concentrated effort into this program than into any other single aspect of college life, and we feel justified in the results. Attendance is required, but seats are not checked and so far this appeal to mature responsibility is succeeding. It is not succeeding 100 percent, but it is better than we dared hope when we began this system a year and a half ago. The result in the lives of the students is sufficient to make us believe the enormous effort is justified.

Naturally a college will have instruction in religion. It will not be impressed by the curious argument of those who say you cannot have religious instruction because of divisions into denominations and faiths. It is to be noted that those who present this argument are not sufficiently consistent to rule out politics or philosophy on the same grounds. If you have men of moral integrity and real objectivity, they can teach religion in such a way that students gain instruction rather than indoctrination. Certainly such instruction is needed, for today few have any clear idea of what they believe and why.

One of the glories of a college is the possibility of deep friendships between scholars devoted to different disciplines, who can gain enormously from what they learn from one another, but often, in our modern institutions, we have failed to take advantage of this. We then cease to be real colleges and become a set of little departments, each going its own way. In the summer of 1939, shortly before he died, I visited Professor Rendell Harris in England. He was the last survivor of that group of scholars who, near the end of the nineteenth century, made Johns Hopkins one of the most exciting places on the face of the earth. I took the opportunity to ask the ancient man what was the secret of that amazing burst of intellectual life. "It was very simple," he said, "we all attended each other's lectures." And then he went on to say how it raised a man's sight to have a scholar like Professor Gildersleeve in the room. I am convinced that we could change much of our college atmosphere if the advice of Rendell Harris were generally followed today.

One reason we cannot do this, or at least think we cannot do this, is that we teach too much. *In the modern college there is too much teaching and not enough learning.* Often the instructor does the work for students when they ought to do it for themselves. We ruin the whole idea when we make it the chief task of a teacher to be a purveyor of information. The information is in *books,* for printing has been invented. The teacher is the enkindler; the best he can do is to light a fire. And the greatness of any college is directly proportioned to the number of teachers who are truly effective in this sacred function. *The greatest college is the college with the best teachers.*

One of the major tragedies in modern college experience is the lack of friendship between students and teachers. It is our open scandal. I have visited many colleges where there is the frank recognition that the community is broken at this vital point. It is our shame that even in our smaller colleges so few real friendships between students and faculty members exist. A good part of the trouble comes from the side of the student who is self-conscious in the presence of the teacher because he fears the accusation of his fellow students that he is apple-polishing. Apple-polishing is not very bad, but the failure to make friendships is bad indeed if what we have said about influence is true. It is bad because education, at its best, is not mere information, but rather the communication of truth through the medium of personality. If some demon wanted to do his worst to hinder our process, this rift is what he would create and perpetuate.

If we are wise, we shall attack this problem at its roots. Much of the trouble arises from the fact that, in our conventional American system of instruction, the same man is both teacher and judge. There is no good reason why this should be so, and much reason why it should not be. One of the best forward steps we could take in our colleges would be in the general introduction of a system of outside examiners. The case for outside examiners lies in the threefold fact that it (a) raises the sights of the student; (b) raises the sights of the instructor; and (c) improves the relationship between the two since they become obvious partners in the effort to help the student to do well.

We could provide a system of outside examiners by pooling our resources in certain areas and thus make a great advance with very little expense. Thus colleges in special areas may move in the direction of the creation of regional universities which perform their first function in the provision of examining boards. Here is a chance for real pioneering in our day. Formerly distance made this impracticable, but now modern transportation has altered the picture radically. In some such way we may finally have the advantages of real colleges and real universities at the same time. One result would be that colleges could begin to have effective and beneficent competition in something besides athletics and debating.

Ours is an exciting job. We know full well that we are in a race with catastrophe and that civilization is in jeopardy, but we are fortunate in that there is something that we can do about it. We can deliberately create little islands of hope in the midst of a century of despair. We are doing what we love most.

The Redemption of the College

This address, "The Redemption of the College," was delivered before a national conference of Christian educators at Williamsburg, Virginia, in June of 1976, as part of the Bicentennial celebration.* This recent address shows that Professor Trueblood's concern for the Christian college is as great as it was when it first possessed his mind. Like "The Idea of a College," this address continues the theme of hope and the need for renewal on the college campus. Toward the close of this essay, Dr. Trueblood offers a fourfold "plan of action," designed to renew the dream of the Christian college. This plan is not easy, but then anything worth saving requires effort. Dr. Trueblood places the challenge before us, but the question remains whether we have the stamina to recover a most important part of our culture.

*National Colloquium on Christian Education, June, 1976, sponsored by the Education Commission of the Southern Baptist Convention.

7
The Redemption of the College

When the Christian college finally emerged in history, it appeared as a genuine novelty. Curiously it appeared, in its fullness, only in the United States of America, and it has never been duplicated. Indeed, in many parts of the world, it is not even understood, much less reproduced. In contemporary Russia there is nothing remotely similar to the Christian college, while in Europe there are only slight approximations to the pattern. Since this particular educational pattern sheds important light upon the character of our national culture, to which it has contributed in a remarkable fashion, the effort to appreciate it is a worthy goal in the Bicentennial year of our country.

Schools are indeed cultural institutions of genuine antiquity. The earliest evidences of civilization always seem to include at least three institutions: a prison, an altar, and a school. As soon as our ancestors became civilized at all, they recognized the necessity of establishing some means of passing on from generation to generation something of what they had learned about the way to live. Consequently, a civilization without some sort of education is clearly a contradiction in terms. In its simplest form, as President Garfield appreciated, it is a log with a teacher on one end of it and a child on the other, for all educational development is an elaboration of this basic and important pattern.

It is helpful to remind ourselves of many steps in educational history. All are indebted, for example, to the embodiment of Plato's dream which was known as the academy. This significant institution of learning lasted for fully nine hundred years until it was finally closed during the reign of Justinian. Plato's pattern was remarkable, chiefly because it not only perpetuated previous learning but also encouraged students to think for themselves, so that culture might be truly progressive. Pupils often advanced by degrees, until they, themselves, were expected to become the tutors of others. No thoughtful person can scratch around among the ruined foundation stones where the academy once flourished, just outside ancient Athens, without deep emotion. We may say with propriety what Samuel Johnson said at Iona in 1773, when, in the company of James Boswell, he visited the famous island off the west coast of Scotland:

> Far from me, and from my friends, be such frigid philosophy as may conduct us indifferent and unmoved over any ground which has been dignified by wisdom, bravery, or virtue. That man is little to be envied, whose patriotism would not gain force upon the plain of *Marathon,* or whose piety would not grow warmer among the ruins of *Iona!*

Just as we are moved by the remembrance of the Athenian academy, we are also moved when we are reminded of the simple beginnings of now famous universities, such as Paris, Oxford, Cambridge, Heidelberg, and Edinburgh. Some of these have now lasted many centuries, but the shadow of none is yet as long as that cast by Plato's dream. The idea of a university, to employ Cardinal Newman's phrase, developed slowly, arising in England by the establishment of separate colleges, all of which were originally ecclesiastical. The original pattern was that deemed appropriate to the education of the priesthood, but, in the ultimate outcome, this became only a minor factor in the total enterprise. Furthermore, in the numerous universities patterned in part upon those developed in the Middle Ages, theological education now has no part at all, the institutions being solely secular and proud of that fact. In some instances all of the major professions are represented in the curriculum, with the exception of that of the public ministry. Thus the academic pendulum has swung from one extreme to the other.

In many countries today the whole of higher education is in the hands of government, being carried on entirely at the expense of the state. This is conspicuously true in the U.S.S.R., where large expenditures for advanced education are made but in which there is no theological education except for a few feeble and vestigial efforts. The notion that the Christian faith can have or ought to have any reasonable part in general education, in the provision of either motivation or content, is looked upon as ridiculous. In countries not controlled by consciously Communist philosophy, the universities tend to be almost equally secularized, but the existence of religious schools, chiefly for the instruction of those devoted to religious vocations, is accepted as a valid part of the total culture, sometimes being supported by government funds.

The Christian college, as it grew to maturity in American culture, was something markedly different from either the secularized university, on the one hand, or the institution for vocational religious training on the other. This point requires careful elaboration because it is frequently missed, especially by strangers who are unfamiliar with American history. Foreigners, when told of our Christian colleges, jump at once to the conclusion that they are devoted to a denominational promotion or to the exclusive training of theologians. This, however, as Americans well know, is very far from the truth. Because of the ease with which misunderstanding may be produced, it is important for us to try to describe again the idea of a Christian college as it developed in the English colonies of America, and as it flourished both in the nineteenth century and in the early twentieth century before significant decay began to appear. It is the root idea which must be understood first, because it is the idea which has been productive of valuable fruits.

The characteristic American educational unit did not appear in the earliest colonial days because the first educational institutions were cultural imports. Harvard College was meant to be essentially a reproduction of Emmanuel College, Cambridge, its original purpose being the production of a trained clergy. At its inception, Harvard did not *have* a divinity school because, in essence,

The Redemption of the College

it *was* a divinity school, though it did not long remain such.

While ministerial training was the first felt need in America, other purposes soon began to dominate the thinking of the English colonists. Scholars were needed in a variety of sciences if the life of the new communities was to prosper. Just as men do not live by bread alone, so they do not live by worship alone. In the eighteenth century the disciplines which we associate with the mind of Benjamin Franklin were gaining in popular favor. The creation of the American Philosophical Society was a crucial step in the determination to encourage all useful kinds of learning. We became aware that we needed not only practitioners of medicine and law but also of astronomy and other sciences if we were to be a truly civilized people. Therefore, there arose laboratories and observatories, as well as libraries and museums.

A significant factor in this spread of interest in learning was the powerful idea that creatures made in the image of God should learn all that they could about his world. If the earth is the Lord's and the fullness thereof, no kind of inquiry is logically off limits. We know something significant about the rationale of the Christian college when we observe the growth of Yale College under the powerful leadership of the first Timothy Dwight. If anyone was ever a committed Christian, President Dwight was, so that, almost singlehanded he altered the mood of the college to which he was so deeply devoted. Far from being antiscientific, Dwight, in pursuing consistently his dominant philosophy, determined to introduce the study of chemistry into Yale College. In this enterprise his success was phenomenal. Under the leadership of Benjamin Silliman, the brilliant young man whom he selected to inaugurate the new discipline, chemistry flourished, thereby providing a model that was widely copied.

The Christian college, as developed on American soil by virtue of many powerful minds, was seldom narrowly denominational, though each successive institution came into being by the thought, effort, and sacrifice of Christian people. Therefore, it is a misnomer to speak of such an institution as *private*. It was, in most instances, just as public as were the new state universities when they finally and belatedly arose because student enrollment was seldom limited on any sectarian basis. The college was public because it was organized for the public good, a point not contradicted by the arrangement of finances, independent of the public purse. Indeed, if we require a descriptive adjective for such a college, "independent" is far more accurate than is "private," but "Christian" is better than either one. The third adjective is more nearly accurate because what America developed providentially was not so much education in specifically Christian subjects, as education, *in all subjects,* from a Christian perspective.

This is the precise point which foreign observers often miss, and which some of our contemporary citizens, never having known the Christian college at its best, do not even now understand. The unity of the Christian college, when it understands itself, is not a unity of curriculum, but a *unity of purpose.* It is a complex unity, involving both studies and the reason for the study. Charles Wesley provided a happy pattern of phrases when he sang: "Unite the pair so long disjoined, knowledge and vital piety."

According to this sophisticated philosophy of education, every subject is worth studying, for no valid discipline is a threat to the rationality of the Christian faith. The student who believes, as did Dwight's students seventy years ago, that the world is God's world, is naturally eager to learn all that he can about such a world. It is not really strange that, during most of the years of the dominance of the Christian college in our culture, the most devout of all of the professors tended to be those in the natural sciences. In Earlham, for example, one of the greatest of its presidents, Joseph Moore, was, in addition to his administrative duties, the one who taught biology and built the museum, at the same time being a recognized minister. The important point to notice is that this conjunction of abilities was not looked upon as odd.

What was the function of the Christian faith in such an educational pattern? It did not, for the most part, dictate the choice of subjects taught and learned. It did, however, determine the mood in which they were taught and provided a powerful motivation for learning. History is more interesting if it is seen as the sum of the ways in which God has dealt with his children, and science is enabled by recognizing that it is a way of thinking

God's thoughts after him. There is no subject that cannot be taught better by the mood of humility. Because it was in a college permeated by such an approach to learning that I began my own higher education, I can never be sufficiently grateful.

Central to such a college is, of course, the experience of worship. It is no accident that, on the characteristic Christian college campus, the chapel building is the central or focal structure and that the chapel bell is the one sound to which all residents respond. It is a great thing for those who learn and also for those who teach to worship regularly together. Here, when it is real, is a genuine antidote to the fragmentation and the trivialization that beset many contemporary educational undertakings. There may be other ways in which the reality of community can be produced, but if so, it is not evident what they are. Community does not come by dictation or merely by being together physically, but primarily by looking together in the same direction.

For those in an educational effort to worship together is one of the most lifting experiences conceivable. It means that time is set aside for what is noble, and that proud persons, kneeling in prayer or singing great hymns, are able to transcend some of their littleness. It is no wonder that we turn again and again to the words which Professor Alfred North Whitehead wrote in 1929, "Moral education is impossible apart from the habitual vision of greatness." When I dined by his side I knew what he meant!

We are dealing now with one of America's original

contributions to world civilization. Most of the pattern, already briefly described, has been developed during the two hundred years in which we have been an independent and separate nation. It is a pattern which deserves to be perpetuated and spread, but, before it can be multiplied or even maintained, it must be clearly understood and appreciated. In this Bicentennial year it is important to realize the extent to which the pattern which has done so much for the world is truly indigenous. When we stress the centrality of the chapel experience, we may be reminded that the ancient colleges of Oxford and Cambridge also had chapels with focal significance architecturally, but the differences produced in America are immense. One difference of importance arises from the fact that, as American culture grew and flourished, the colleges were established, not in a few clusters, but in deliberately separated locations. Each came to be a center of light miles away from others and often the only bright spot in the cultural wilderness. The students, with their laboratories, their observatories, and their chapels, had the opportunity to know what it means to maintain standards in both learning and conduct. The spacing, though largely unintended, had the beneficent effect of providing cultural strong points where they were most needed, often influencing thereby the development of entire areas of a very broad land.

The fact that the love of God and the love of learning could coexist did great things for many minds. A large proportion of our leaders during the two centuries of our history have been nourished in precisely such centers.

Without the emergence of the Christian college, the history of the United States of America might have been good, but it could not have been the same.

The sad and uncontested fact is that the vision of the Christian college is now dimmed. Though a few institutions have maintained the integrity of the vision in both theory and practice, these now constitute a minority. In the majority, the major features already described are today conspicuously absent. The chapel, far from being central in fact as well as architecture, is often empty. The spring is dry! Sometimes there is a supposed continuity, with worship being conducted, but it is no longer for the entire academic community; frequently we find a dozen where once there were a thousand. Some reference to biblical studies is maintained but without genuine emphasis because it is without requirement. The combination of Christian commitment and scholarly achievement, once the standard, has been either neglected or consciously abandoned in hundreds of colleges. One consequence is a general lowering of standards. Now in a frantic effort to maintain a supposedly desirable level of enrollment, entrance standards are being lowered.

The moral level is often so lax that what emerges is almost total permissiveness. Many, including some teaching faculty, do not uphold the idea of chastity, but opt, instead, for something which they call the new morality. When this is examined with any intellectual rigor, it is very hard to see that it means anything at all, unless it means the complete absence of any objective moral order. It is said, in defense, that the college, in this regard, is

The Redemption of the College

not to blame, since this is the way the contemporary society operates. The notion that the college should challenge the world's ways, rather than accept them with acquiescence, seems not to be seriously entertained. By condoning the loss of standards, the college has nothing left except tolerance, which turns out to be the weakest of all of the virtues.

The most obvious phase of decline, so far as the impartial observer is concerned, is that of aesthetic standards, whether in dress, dining, or manners. Thousands now go through the entire college courses without a single experience of dignified dining and many graduate without having learned the most elemental rules of mannerly behavior. It is widely affirmed that slovenly dress has nothing to do with character, but that this is true is far from self-evident. Indeed there is plenty of evidence to show that slovenly dress, or conscious ugliness, really affects the person at a deep level. How strange that the very institutions for which people have sacrificed, in the hope of raising the cultural level, should now themselves become the enemies of culture. What if the intended cure becomes one of the clearest indications of the disease? There are certainly colleges in which, by almost any standard which can be devised, life is made worse rather than better. Some become addicted to drugs because of the pressures felt in college, which might not have been felt equally in the world outside. The pressures which lead to unchastity are really greater in some college communities than they are in the homes from which the students come. Is it any real wonder, therefore, that thousands of decent people now are beginning to question the wisdom of the enormous financial sacrifice which college entails. The saddest part of this picture is that the revulsion has come, not merely against secular education, but even more against that kind which was originated and long supported by the church of Jesus Christ.

What has been said is demonstrably true, but it is not the whole truth. The other and, in the long run, the most important part of the truth is that renewal is still possible. Every student of history realizes that civilization can go down, and this he knows because so many springs have gone dry. In producing his monumental work, Gibbon made every literate person understand this terrible fact. Rome *did* decay, and so can we. For a generation, we have pondered the possibility of the decline of the West, and, if we are honest, we have to admit that this is more than an empty phrase. But the other side of the matter is that renewal is a genuine option for any people. Indeed, ours is a world in which there can be a new shoot in the old stump. But renewal is never automatic! It comes only when people face their failure boldly, admitting their mistakes, and take the requisite steps to allow the processes of renewal to operate. If we refuse to face the fact of decline, there is no hope at all.

I am among those who believe that the fair dream which we call the Christian college is still a live option for modern men and women. Some colleges may, indeed, be in such terrible decay that it is a waste of time to bother with them. In short, some of them may be the

The Redemption of the College

barren fig trees, of which Jesus spoke in a moving parable (Luke 3:7-9), and consequently, it is reasonable to let them die and be cut down. But these constitute only a small minority. For many, and especially for the colleges which the people in my Williamsburg audience deeply love, the point of no return has not yet been reached. But the situation is urgent and time will not wait. Our Christian task, therefore, is to use our minds to try to present and to follow a program of renewal. What is it?

As I have thought long about the situation of the Christian college in America, recognizing both the magnitude of the conception and the sorrow of its decline, I have turned to the words of Abraham Lincoln when he said on December 1, 1862, "We shall nobly save, or meanly lose, the last best hope of earth." I do not say that the Christian college is the last best hope, but I do say that it is part of that hope. I want, while I am alive, to give my best thought to the elaboration of the redemptive idea, to face honestly our departure from it, and to assist wherever possible, in its renewal. I think that renewal is possible! My reason for thinking this is the observation that, though some institutions may have decayed so much that revival is, humanly speaking, improbable, there are, at the same time, many in which a genuine ground of hope remains. There are institutions in which the decline is not yet fatal and in which there are loyal persons ready to give new embodiment to the dream. There are, I believe, numerous such persons at Williamsburg this very day.

What we need now is a concrete plan of action. To this end I now outline a fourfold program, in the conviction that each of the four proposals is necessary.

1. We must accept our uniqueness. If we suppose that we are engaged in education in general or that we are trying, in each instance, to maintain just another college, we are almost certain to fail. The tax-supported institution is bound to do better if mere education is what is attempted. Our success lies in the frank acceptance of a unique vocation, providing thereby a valid option which the wholly secularized institution is not free to provide. We can study values, not in some abstract inquiry, but in the conviction that we are dealing with an objective moral order, which is consistent with the biblical revelation. We believe that we are examining, not merely what we happen to prefer, but what is objectively true. As a Christian is one who is committed to Jesus Christ, so a Christian college is an institution of higher learning in which the Christian revelation provides the major premise for the entire intellectual operation. Like Archimedes, we need *a place to stand* if we expect to move the world, and the genuine Christian college has precisely such a place. This, as any thoughtful person realizes, doesn't automatically solve all of our problems, but it does something better; it provides an alternative to a hopeless relativism. The Christian college recognizing its own inherent strength will not find survival simple or easy, but it will be on the way.

2. We must accept, unapologetically, the principle of requirement. Because all of us are aware of erosion at this very point, we may now be ready to say what is required and to stand by it with courage. When we examine the issue with any care, it is hard to see why any intelligent person ever supposed that requirements could be abandoned with impunity. Believing, as I do, in medical education, I am not ashamed to say that I shall try to select a physician who has had to meet requirements in medical school, rather than doing his own thing. A doctor who has been allowed to evade requirements is clearly a social menace.

If requirement is a valid principle, we can reject permissiveness and reject it unequivocally. That permissiveness is a disease which has infected contemporary education is obvious to any candid observer. Tired of standing up under constant pressure, teachers and administrators have tried to solve their problem by unconditional surrender. Sometimes an effort is made to defend surrender as a virtue in that it enlarges the area of freedom. Each student is benefited, so the argument goes, in that he is liberated to do what he really wants to do. Some administrators announce, with evident pride, rather than with shame, that they no longer operate *in loco parentis.* This use of the Latin tongue may at first seem impressive, but on examination, it turns out to be capitulation, which of course is easier than struggle, but which leads to defeat for everyone. The renunciation of any parental role means that the only part of living for which responsibility is accepted is one of decreasing importance. The false appeal of the position arises from the assumption that an obsolete stand is being rejected, leading to a new and brighter day. The difficulty with this is that it is not true.

As almost all who examine the concept of permissiveness soon recognize, the way of absolute freedom is that of absolute destruction of civilization. For one thing, it is intrinsically self-destructive because it destroys the freedom of others. If I demand the freedom to play loud music at all times, I thereby destroy, on the part of my neighbors, the freedom to sleep. Because the evils of permissiveness have become apparent, those who still practice it frequently seek to avoid the use of the word. There are many actions which in a decent civilization will not be tolerated. Whatever our method of recovery may be, we shall not be saved by softness.

3. We must be sincerely devoted to excellence. Because mediocrity invades us on every side, there must be concerted effort to maintain standards. One of the saddest features of the current academic scene is grade inflation. There are courses, in supposedly reputable institutions, in which the lowest grade, in actual practice, is B. We do not need to think very long to realize that an A is less valuable when nearly all students achieve this level. If anyone has the naivete to claim that the high grades are given because the students deserve them or that people are smarter than they used to be, he will be laughed at as he deserves to be.

The important point to make now is that, in the restoration of standards of excellence, the church college is potentially in a strong position. Though we are public, we are also independent. We have, accordingly, the right to uphold a high standard in admissions, in advancement, and in graduation. We are not in the entertainment business! We can maintain graduation by achievement and not merely by the accumulation of credits in easy subjects. We can require study in both logic and ethics if we think that they are necessary for the accomplishment of our magnificent purpose. We can employ outside examiners, thus avoiding the danger involved when the teacher is the sole judge of his own product. This may be difficult to introduce in the state institution, but the Christian college has the freedom to innovate for the sake of excellence.

Part of our purpose is the production of Christian intellectuals, men and women who can combine the love of God with the love of learning. If this is not done in the way of excellence, it will not be done at all. The option provided by the existence of the Christian college should be harder rather than easier, when compared with its alternatives, for we are in a more ambitious enterprise than are our competitors. This, however, is something which we have sometimes failed to realize, but unless we recognize it, we shall not survive and furthermore, we shall not deserve to survive.

4. We must reinstate the vision of wholeness. It is extremely easy to promote an education that is fragmented. Thus, it is possible today for a Ph.D. degree to be awarded to a person in a narrow field of inquiry, so that the recipient has very little acquaintance with the history of ideas or of great literature. The Christian college has a unique opportunity, in this regard, to demonstrate a vision of wholeness in marked contrast to the general procedure. As Christian educators we affirm the necessity of a number of values, and we believe that they can be nourished together, *better than in separation.*

Is it too much to expect of a college graduate that he or she should be able to speak the English language not only with clarity but also with some distinction and elegance? Is it wrong to suppose that college people should be able to avoid the constant employment of poor grammar? I realize, of course, that we hear barbarisms every day, particularly in television broadcasts, but a good argument can be made for the conviction that a college ought to challenge the prevailing culture, rather than to reflect it. Is it a strange expectation that college educated persons should be able to stand upon their feet and to speak a few sentences that are articulate, without constant humming and hawing? Is it unreasonable to think that college people should be able to write simple letters that can be understood and even to spell the words correctly? If the colleges are not producing such persons, from where will they come? While the Christian college is devoted to academic excellence, it is also devoted to courtesy, to disciplined living, and to good manners. The way people learn to dine may be as important as the way in which they learn to perform chemical experiments. Few practices are more civilizing than that of grace before meals. This is, indeed, one of the ways in which we rise above the level of animality. All recognize that this sort of civilized behavior may be difficult to institute in a frankly secularized institution, but it ought to be possible to encourage it unapologetically in any Christian college.

The good life always comes by a combination, but this is nothing new to Christians who have any genuine understanding of their classical position. Over and over we return to the words of Christ, "I came that they may have life, and have it abundantly" (John 10:10). Here is our standard: The abundant life includes both rigorous thinking and courteous behavior, both the appreciation of beauty and the concern for one another, both the ability to play and the desire to pray. What we reject, and reject emphatically, is the supposition that, between any of these, it is required of us that we choose. We do not need to choose! The holy conjunction is "and," a word the significance of which is far out of proportion to its size. We can have instructors who are both reverent and scholarly; we can have students who are both genteel and competent; we can have societies which are both liberated and disciplined.

The dream which possesses us is truly a noble one. "Methinks," said Milton, "I see in my mind a noble and puissant nation rousing herself like a strong man after sleep, and shaking her invincible locks." The task before us is not easy, but perhaps, like Milton, we were made for whatever is arduous. There is nothing wrong with the dream. The question is whether we have that devotion sufficient to give it *embodiment*.

# Religious Poetry

8
Religious Poetry

Few persons know about another aspect of Dr. Trueblood's abilities. He is widely known as a philosopher and historian, but few recognize him as a writer of poetry. Indeed he is, and I have selected three of his most inspirational pieces to conclude this work. The hymn "Baptism by Fire" is being widely used in a number of hymnals. Other hymns are promised soon.

At the back of this volume is a complete list of Professor Trueblood's books. These thirty-one volumes are signposts along this philosopher's way. From *The Essence of Spiritual Religion,* his first book, to *While It Is Day,* his last, the perpetual vision of greatness remains a vital part of Professor Trueblood's pilgrimage. Through his books he is helping to light the way for others who are seeking greater spiritual depth in their lives. This is the purpose of this book, and I trust this purpose is being realized.

Baptism by Fire

(1966)

Thou, whose purpose is to kindle:
Now ignite us with Thy fire;
While the earth awaits Thy burning
With Thy passion us inspire.
Overcome our sinful calmness,
Rouse us with redemptive shame;
Baptize with Thy fiery Spirit,
Crown our lives with tongues of flame.

Thou, who in Thy holy Gospel,
Wills that man should truly live:
Make us sense our share of failure,
Our tranquility forgive.
Teach us courage as we struggle
In all liberating strife!
Lift the smallness of our vision,
By Thine own abundant life.

Thou, who still a sword delivers,
Rather than a placid peace:
With Thy sharpened word disturb us,
From complacency, release!
Save us now from satisfaction,
When we privately are free,
Yet are undisturbed in spirit,
By our brother's misery.

New Pentecost

A Hymn for Contemporary Christians
(1977)

Accept, O Lord, our gratitude
    For Pentecost of old;
That miracle of burning hearts
    Which Christ Himself foretold.

Rebuke the mildness of our faith;
    Forgive the careless act,
Teach us, again, to love and dream;
    Make Pentecost a fact!

Grant us a vision bold and new,
    The courage now to share,
Enlarge our fellowship in Him,
    Through Whom we learn to care.

Restore, we pray, the vision clear
    Of what Thy Church could be;
Vouchsafe to us the potent dream
    Begin, today, with me!

Being written in common meter, this hymn can be sung to *St. Ann,* perhaps the best known hymn tune in the modern world. The author of the music is William Croft, once organist of Westminster Abbey. Though long associated, in the public mind, with the words of Isaac Watts, "Our God Our Help in Ages Past," there is no good reason why the noble music should be limited to one set of words.

Ten Commandments for Children *

Above all else love God alone;
> bow down to neither wood nor stone.

God's name refuse to take in vain;
> the sabbath rest with care maintain.

Respect your parents all your days;
> hold sacred human life always.

Be loyal to your chosen mate;
> steal nothing, neither small nor great.

Keep to the truth in word and deed,
> and rid your mind of selfish greed.

* Published in *Foundations For Reconstruction* (New York: Harper and Row, 1946), p. 10.

Benediction

Go in joy;
Sin no more,
Love God,
Serve the brethren.

Books by D. Elton Trueblood

The Essence of Spiritual Religion	Harper and Brothers	1936
The Trustworthiness of Religious Experience	Allen and Unwin	1939
The Knowledge of God	Harper and Brothers	1939
The Logic of Belief	Harper and Brothers	1942
The Predicament of Modern Man	Harper and Brothers	1944
Dr. Johnson's Prayers	Harper and Brothers	1947
Foundations for Reconstruction	Harper and Brothers	1946
Alternative to Futility	Harper and Brothers	1948
The Common Ventures of Life	Harper and Brothers	1949
The Signs of Hope in a Century of Despair	Harper and Brothers	1950
The Life We Prize	Harper and Brothers	1951
Your Other Vocation	Harper and Brothers	1952
The Recovery of Family Life (with Pauline Trueblood)	Harper and Row	1953
Declaration of Freedom	Harper and Brothers	1955
Philosophy of Religion	Harper and Brothers	1957
The Yoke of Christ	Harper and Brothers	1958
The Idea of a College	Harper and Brothers	1959
Confronting Christ	Harper and Brothers	1960
The Company of the Committed	Harper and Brothers	1961

General Philosophy	Harper and Row	1963
The Humor of Christ	Harper and Row	1964
The Lord's Prayers	Harper and Row	1965
The People Called Quakers	Harper and Row	1966
The Incendiary Fellowship	Harper and Row	1967
Robert Barclay	Harper and Row	1968
A Place to Stand	Harper and Row	1969
The New Man for Our Time	Harper and Row	1970
The Future of the Christian	Harper and Row	1971
The Validity of the Christian Mission	Harper and Row	1972
Abraham Lincoln: Theologian of American Anguish	Harper and Row	1973
While It Is Day: An Autobiography	Harper and Row	1974